ZULU TERROR

THE MFECANE HOLOCAUST 1815–1840

ROBIN BINCKES

Pen & Sword
MILITARY

A female Zulu *nyanga*, or shaman. (Wellcome Images)

First published in Great Britain in 2019 by
PEN AND SWORD MILITARY
an imprint of
Pen and Sword Books Ltd
47 Church Street
Barnsley
South Yorkshire S70 2AS

ISBN 978 1 52672 889 0

Maps by George Anderson
Front cover painting by Craig Bone
Typeset by Aura Technology and Software Services, India
Printed and bound by TJ International Ltd, Padstow, Cornwall

Pen & Sword Books Ltd incorporates the imprints of Pen & Sword
Archaeology, Atlas, Aviation, Battleground, Discovery, Family History, History, Maritime, Military,
Naval, Politics, Railways, Select, Social History, Transport, True Crime, Claymore Press, Frontline
Books, Leo Cooper, Praetorian Press, Remember When, Seaforth Publishing and Wharncliffe.

For a complete list of Pen and Sword titles please contact
Pen and Sword Books Limited
47 Church Street, Barnsley, South Yorkshire, S70 2AS, England
email: enquiries@pen-and-sword.co.uk
website: www.pen-and-sword.co.uk

CONTENTS

N

ZAMBEZI R.

SALISBURY

BULAWAYO

RHODESIA
(ZIMBABWE)

MOZAMBIQUE

SWAKOPMUND

WINDHOEK

BOTSWANA

SOUTH WEST
AFRICA
(NAMIBIA)

Transvaal

Tropic of Capricorn

NELSPRUIT

PRETORIA

JOHANNESBURG

MAPUTO
(LOURENÇO MARQUES)

SWAZILAND

KIMBERLEY

Orange
Free State

Natal

BLOEMFONTEIN

PIETERMARITZBURG

LESOTHO

DURBAN

SOUTH AFRICA

Cape Province

CAPE TOWN

PORT ELIZABETH

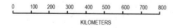

0   100   200   300   400   500   600   700   800

KILOMETERS

Southern Africa in a late 20th-century context. (Genevieve Edwards)

INTRODUCTION

The Mfecane (scatterings or crushings) raged for a period of some forty years as a giant convulsion of conflict that swept Southeast Africa from the end of the eighteenth century to about 1840. Much debated and argued by historians—the reasons for the causes are still searched for today—the Mfecane resulted in the deaths of hundreds of thousands; how many is unlikely to ever be established, though some put the figure at close to two million. Suffice to say that people were killed on a genocidal scale, villages destroyed and hundreds of thousands of cattle, goats and sheep plundered. It led to the formation of new nations with the effects of the Mfecane still felt today.

The epicenter of the Mfecane was KwaZulu-Natal where at the turn of the nineteenth century more than eighty clans of the Nguni people existed. Over the next forty years some remained small while others, usually dependent on the aspirations

Cape Point, the southernmost tip of the Cape of Good Hope. (Zaian)

of their leaders and their quest for power, turned on their neighbours and, in the same way as large corporates take over smaller businesses today, gobbled up the weaker clans. In many instances members of the defeated clans subjugated themselves to the aggressor—*khonza'd*—while others fled, and to survive, attacked and looted their neighbors stimulating a massive chain reaction that eventually encompassed the whole of Southeast Africa. As the conflicts intensified, the fleeing clans spilled over the Drakensberg onto the lands of the Highveld beyond where like collapsing dominos they fell upon each other. If fingers should be pointed at individuals who played a major role in destabilizing the subcontinent they are Senzakhona, Shaka, Dingane, Matiwane, Mantatisi and Mzilikazi

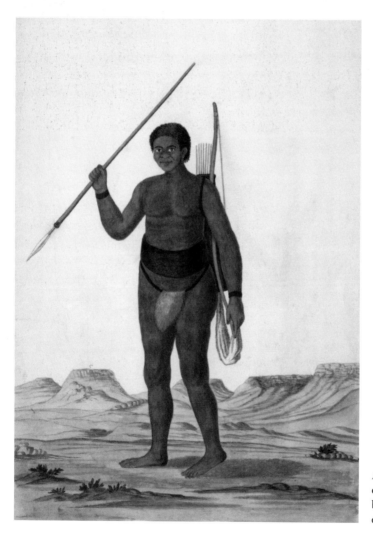

A Bushman at the Cape of Good Hope, a sketch by Johannes Schemaker, c. 1776

Zulu women brewing beer. (J. S. & A. P. Bergh)

There were four major theatres of war: KwaZulu Natal where the Zulu nation grew from the seeds of the Mfecane; the northern frontier where conflict grew between the Griqua (people of mixed race) and local tribes exacerbated by the intrusion of the Europeans who were beginning to move out of the Cape Colony to escape British control; the Drakensberg hinterland where the spillover effects of refugees from rampaging tribes were felt; and the eastern frontier—the Eastern Cape—where European encroachment had led to a century of warfare with the Xhosa nation.

In Natal, Dingiswayo had established trading links with the Portuguese at Delgoa Bay (where Maputo, capital of Mozambique, is today sited). Most of this trade was in ivory and he jealously protected his trading rights against other clans in the region. Towards the end of the eighteenth century it is estimated that over 100,000 pounds of ivory (the equivalent of 4,000 elephant killings) a year were being exported. Hunters of all hues and origins scoured the interior. Slave trade at that time was being undertaken, mainly with Brazil as the end destination; however Delagoa Bay was not the major export port of slaves from Mozambique but Inhambane farther north. As early as 1719 slaves had been taken from Natal by the slaver *Mercury* where it is recorded 74 boys and girls were bought. These slaves ended up in Virginia; however, again, like

Voortrekkers move north into the hinterland of the sub-continent. (G. S. Smithard & J. R. Skelton)

Delagoa Bay, slaving was sporadic and there was no steady stream of slaves that indi-cated a flourishing slave trade. On the east coast of Africa, that honour went to the Arabs farther north who were slaving on an unprecedented scale out of present-day Mombasa, Dar es Salaam and Tanga, into the Middle East, the Near East, the Gulf and the Far East

In the area around Delagoa Bay the Thembe soon became the dominant tribe after defeating and then absorbing several minor tribes. They jealously guarded the trade routes in the area.[1] By the turn of the nineteenth century corn had replaced other forms of crops such as millet and sorghum. The quest for land was exacerbated in the early years of the nineteenth century by drought. The first drought struck in 1802 and was called the *Madlathule*, meaning 'Eat what you can and keep quiet'. Again in 1812 and in the years between 1816 and 1818 the lack of rain forced the tribes to expand their areas of grazing, giving added impetus to the clashes between tribes as each sought to strengthen their own position by increasing their spheres of influence,[2] and, of course, they were starving.

1. THE ARRIVAL OF THE SETTLERS

On 3 December 2017 Chief Khoisan SA accompanied by fellow marchers Brendon Billings and Shane Plaatjies set up camp on the lawns of the Union Buildings in Pretoria after having walked for three weeks from Port Elizabeth to Pretoria, a distance of 700 miles, to demand recognition of their language and culture from Jacob Zuma, the president of South Africa. Five hundred additional marchers joined the three men that day to add their voices to those of the three Khoisan marchers.

South Africa boasts the Cradle of Humankind, the site of the first controlled use of fire, the fossils of Australopithecus Africanis, Mrs Ples (2.6–2.8 million years old), Naledi (over 3 million years old) and Little Foot (3.67 million years old). It also boasts the oldest living people on the planet: the Khoisan. Indisputably

Sebastian Munster's map of Africa, c. 1535. (*Cosmographiae Universalis*, Basle, 1640)

9

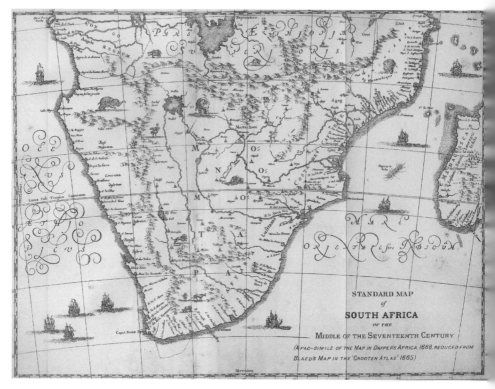

Southourn Africa, Blaeu's 1665 map.

the Khoisan are the indigenous people of southern Africa with their origins dating back to the early mists of time.

Consisting of five major groups—the KhoeKhoen, San, Nama, Korana and later, after the arrival of the white man, the Griqua—all of these groups speak the language of Khoekhoegowab, which consists mainly of 'clicks' and sounds made by the use of the tongue with very few guttural sounds.[1] The KhoeKhoen and San in turn each broke down into many subclans, nineteen for the KhoeKhoen including the Cochoqua, Chainouqua, Hessequa, Inqua, Gona, Hoengeyqua. The KhoeKhoen were pastoralists, owned cattle and were nomadic to a certain extent while the San were hunter-gatherers and also nomadic.

The early European settlers referred to the Khoekoen as Hottentots (also known as Khoikhoi), naming them after the clicking sounds they made when conversing and the San as Bushman. Over the years wars, genocide, smallpox and other diseases brought by the Europeans have all but totally annihilitaed these peoples.

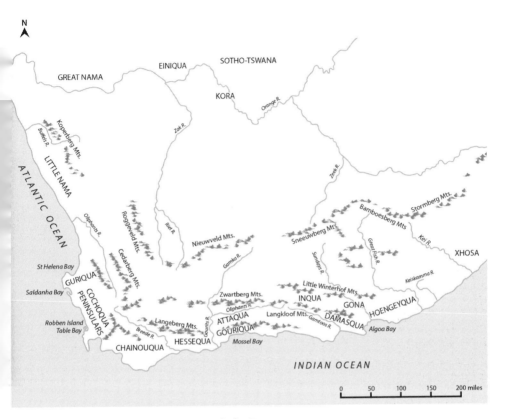

Location of the Khoikhoi before contact with the Europeans.

In neighbouring South West Africa (now Nambia), which was administered by South Africa as a League of Nations mandate from 1918 until 1990 it was legal to hunt a Bushman up until 1936.

These groups lived in relative harmony until, from about 300 AD, when like a stone being thrown into a pool of still water; this harmony was disturbed by the arrival of the first black people, the Bantu, who originated in the Niger basin of West Africa. Over a period of centuries these people moved down Africa in two distinct streams. Into the interior of southern Africa came the Sotho-speaking people and down the east coast of southern Africa, the Nguni-speaking people.

Seeking better pastures for their cattle the Nguni people reached a river beyond which the grazing was not suitable (today named the Fish river), causing them to stop their wanderings, and it was here, east of the Fish river in the land bounded by the sea and the great Drakensberg mountains that the Nguni people settled.

Prior to becoming separate nations Nguni society was comprised of a myriad of clans or subtribes, ruled by chiefs and subchiefs (*indunas*).

By the beginning of the nineteenth century there were at least forty-six different clans living between the Pongola river in the east and the Umzimkulu river in the west and bounded by the Drakensberg mountains. The largest of these clans were the emaHlutshini (8,208), Ngcobo (8,208) Qwabe (7,182), Ndwandwe (4,104), Mtetwa (4,104). The Zulu were a relatively small clan of 2,052.[2]

There were three major tribes occupying the areas now known as Nquthu Babanango, Empangeni, Mtubatuba, Hlabisa, Nongama, Pongola, Vryheid Melmoth and Mahlabathini. These were the Ngwane, the Ndwandwe and the Mtetwa. West of the Umzimkulu river more Nguni clans existed who later molded themselves into the Pondo, Thembu and Xhosa.

It was here, around 1670, east of the Umzikulu river near the Mhlatuse valley that we first meet Malandela, an Nguni, son of Luzulmane. It is believed that he was from the now non-extant Ntsele clan, which had settled in the eBabanango hills.[3] At this time Malandela took his family and trekked west to the coast. In pouring rain Malandela and his family marched down the left bank of the Mfule river until a suitable place was found to cross the raging torrent. Some of the family, slower to move, stayed behind despite the cold and hungry members of the party who had crossed with Malandela shouting back across the river that they had found a field of delicious fat plants, *izimBece* (wild melons). Those that remained behind chose to settle where they had stopped and built huts and in time became a separate clan, aba-s-emaNgadini ('Those among the watermelons') ruled by Yabana, son of Ngema.

Malandela's party pushed on. Some ten miles farther near the iNkwenkwe hill they crossed the Mhlatuze river and there, under the emaNdawe hill at the end of the valley Malandela built his hut. It was here that Malandela died, leaving his wife Nozinja (Mrs Dogs) and two sons, Qwabe, the eldest, and Zulu. Legend has it that Qwabe coveted the cattle that Nozinja had accumulated by her hard work and shrewdness. When Qwabe attempted to wheedle the cattle from his mother her response was "*Hawu!* And you the heir to all your father's cattle? What then is my child Zulu to receive?" She then abandoned Qwabe and returned inland, accompanied by Zulu and a servant, Mpungose, a man of the Gwabini clan.

After leaving the Mhlatuze valley the small party crossed the river, climbed the hills and headed for the mid-Mfule valley, following a stream and ascending the Mtonjaneni heights. They looked down on the landscape below: stony veld sprinkled with candelabra euphorbias and thorny mimosa scrub, which teemed with wild game of all sorts: elephant, lion, giraffe, buffalo, and thousands of buck. This was to be the home of the aba-kwa Zulu clan. While Zulu settled at Mkumbane, the abandoned brother, Qwabe, lived some thirty miles away, on the lower Mhlatuze river[4] closer to the sea. Here he founded the Qwabe clan. As Nozinja and her small party were seeking a new home so were other smaller groups splitting away and establishing new residences, which would grow into separate clans over time. The two most important clans in the area were the Amangwane and the Mtetwa led by Jama. After the death of Jama two of his sons, Godongwana and Mawewe, vied for the chieftainship resulting in Godongwana fleeing to the Phate stream below Mthonjaneni mountains in the southwest. Here, assisted by Ndlovu of the Mphungose people, they killed Mawewe, cutting him down on the slopes of Sihlungo hill, near Banango.[5] Godongwana came to power as chief of the Mtetwa in 1780. He immediately changed his name to Dingiswayo, or 'One in distress'. Dingiswayo had, as a young man, been forced to flee from his people for a period of time due to jealousy of his right to take over as chief. During this time it is believed that he travelled far to the west and experienced first-hand the military tactics being applied by the British against the Xhosa on the Fish

Clan.	Ratio.	Population.	Clan.	Ratio.	Population.
Zulu	2	2052	Mkwânazi	½	513
Butélezi	2	2052	emDletsheni	½	513
eziBisini	½	513	emaNcubeni	½	513
Dlamini (Butélezi)	½	513	emaNzimeleni	½	513
Sibiya	1	1026	Sokûlu	½	513
Zungu	1	1026	Mbônambi	½	513
emaMbâténi	2	2052	Dube	1	1026
emaQungebeni	½	513	Mbôkazi	½	513
emaÑtshalini	1	1026	Mtêtwá	4	4104
Kûmalo	2	2052	ebaTênjini	2	2052
Mabaso	1	1026	emaNgâdini	½	513
Kôza	1	1026	Xulu	½	513
emaHlutshini	8	8208	êLangeni	2	2052
emaNgwâneni	4	4104	Mpungose	½	513
emaNgwêni	½	513	Magúbane	½	513
Mazibuko	½	513	Sitôle	½	513
Ximba	½	513	emaCûnwini	2	2052
Ndwandwe	4	4104	emaBomvini	1	1026
emaLangeni (Gumede)	2	2052	eMbô	3	3078
Nibele	½	513	Ngcobo	8	8208
Msane	½	513	emaCubeni	½	513
emaNcwangeni	½	513	Lutûli	½	513
Mnqobokazi	½	513	Qwabe	7	7182
			Total		74,898

Clans inhabiting Zululand about 1816, from A. T. Bryant's *Olden Times in Zululand and Natal* (1929). The precision is staggering.

river. Gifted with a superior intellect, Dingiswayo proved to be an enlightened leader, opening up trade in ivory with the Portuguese in Delagoa Bay. He also became the first of the chiefs to introduce the system of regiments, or *impis*, by dividing his followers into battle groups, distinguishing each by name and colour of their shields.[6] He appointed officers of various grades to command them and introduced war dresses to distinguish the officers from the rank and file. It was he who introduced the stabbing spear. He began declaring war on all his neighbouring clans on the pretext that he wished to do away with the constant rivalry and bickering between them. The first to be defeated were the Amakwadini. He directed that the cattle of the Amakwadini be brought to his place of residence. He distributed the oxen to his warriors as a reward for their victory and gave the cows back to the defeated Amakwadini after they had *khonza'*d, accepting his authority over them. In this same way he defeated the Kwabi, AmaLanga, AmaKwadini, AmaZulu, AmaTyaleni, Telayiza, Kuyivane, AmaThembu, AmaSwazi,and Amakose. The only tribe he had not defeated was the Ndwandwe under Chief Zwide. The Mfecane, or crushings, had begun.

Of these early Zulu rulers very little is known. Zulu became the first king of the Zulus until 1709, followed by Punga and then Mageba.[7] Mageba was succeeded by Ndaba and he by Jama who died in 1781. Jama had a number of children including daughters Mnkabayi, Mawa, Mthembase and Mmama, and sons Sojisa, Khekhe, Magunza, Nomaphikela, Nobongoza, Nkwelo and Senzangakhona.

Having been defeated by Dingiswayo, the Zulu under Senzakhona became Dingiswayo's subjects and had to abide by his laws. One of these laws—the custom of circumcision prevalent among the Nguni people—was ceased until Dingiswayo had conquered all around him. It was customary that no intercourse was permitted until after circumcision. Senzakhona had to toe the line. One of the women of the Langeni[8] tribe, Nandi, was selected by Senzakhona as one of the women whom he would one day bed, when he was allowed to, after being circumcised. But Senzakhona became impatient and could not wait for Dingiswayo's go-ahead and had intercourse with Nandi. He impregnated her and Dingiswayo, when noticing the change in Nandi's figure, thought she was suffering from a stomach disease known as *cheka*. The son who was born a few months later, around 1787, became known as Shaka. When the boy was seven years old, Nandi returned to her people, the Langeni. Shaka's maternal grandmother played a large role in raising the boy. He experienced great unhappiness as a child, the young boys in the Langeni tribe continuing to taunt and bully him in exactly the same manner as the young Zulu boys had done in his earlier years. This physical and mental abuse no doubt left its mark, turning a proud and confident young boy into one who was withdrawn, angry and vindictive.

A Hottentot couple, from a 1745 engraving by N. Parr.

After being involved in a fight with the family of a boy who had angered him, Nandi and Shaka left the Langeni and settled briefly among the Qwabe before joining the Mtetwa people. Shaka placed himself under the watchful eye of Chief Jobe of the Mtetwa. When Jobe died in about 1807 his successor, Dingiswayo— Shaka's conception long since forgotten—took over responsibility for raising the boy and placed Shaka under the special care and protection of Ngomane kaMqoboli, one of his chief military commanders and advisors.[9] Nandi returned to her own people, the Langeni, leaving Shaka behind. She later married a commoner and had a son, Engwade. Dingiswayo, having himself been an outcast, had taken pity on the young Shaka and adopted him as his foster son. Shaka grew up very much influenced by Dingiswayo and at an early age served in Dingiswayo's army and participated in many of his campaigns against his neighbours. Shaka became conspicuous by his bravery in battle and soon earned the name of Sigiti, 'We do not dance'.

2. SHAKA: THE QUEST FOR POWER

When Senzakhona, Shaka's father, died in 1816,[1] Shaka approached Dingiswayo and requested that he be appointed chief of the Zulus who were now part of Dingiswayo's growing empire. Dingiswayo refused and informed him that the rightful heir to the Zulu chieftainship was Shaka's half-brother, Umfogazi. Undeterred, Shaka set about removing this obstacle. He employed his younger half-brother, Engwade, the son of Nandi by a commoner, to murder Umfogazi, a task he successfully completed. After the death, Shaka dressed in his war dress and accompanied by many of Dingiswayo's followers, marched into his foster father's kraal chanting a song which he had written extolling his own military prowess. The young bull, Shaka, was beginning to challenge the old bull, Dingiswayo, and Shaka, despite their relationship and his years of loyalty, decided that the time would soon come to remove him.

Shaka, king of the Zulu, from a sketch by Lieutenant James King, a Port Natal merchant.

Four major powers were evolving in the region: the Mabhudu chiefdom in what is now southern Mozambique, the Ndwandwe to the southwest of them between the Mkhuze and Black Mfolozi rivers, the Mtetwa to their south between the lower Mfolozi and the Mhlatuze, and the Qwabe between the Tugela (Thukela) and Mhlatuze rivers. Each of these had developed the *amabutho* system of forming regiments in their armies based on age and had established a form of centralized power. The continuing quest for power, cattle and land caused a ripple effect that grew to be a tidal wave of violence that soon engulfed the region. The rivalry between the Ndwandwe expanding south across the Mkhuze river and the Mtetwa pushing west up the

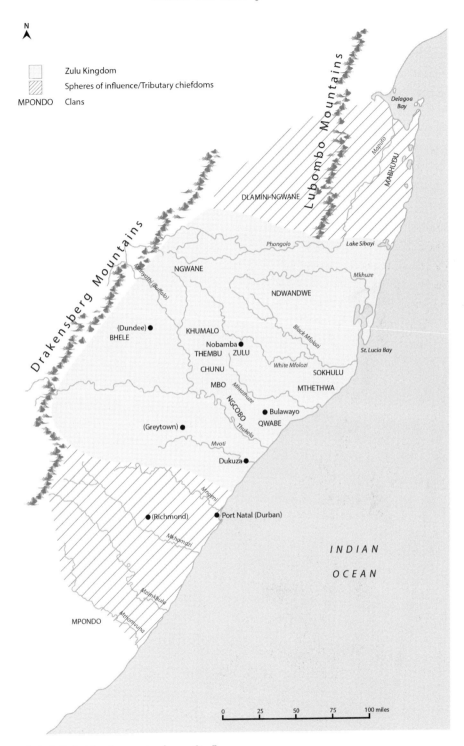

Shaka's Zulu kingdom and sphere of influence.

valley of the White Mfolozi affected the whole area. Constant fighting between the
Ndwandwe and the Mtetwa, for cattle which translated into the need for more grazing
and that in turn for more land, affected the entire constellation of neighboring tribes.
It was the Ndwandwe cattle raids that started off the ripple effect which would
become known as the Mfecane as clan after clan was displaced and who in turn displaced subclan after subclan.[2]

A Hlubi youth.

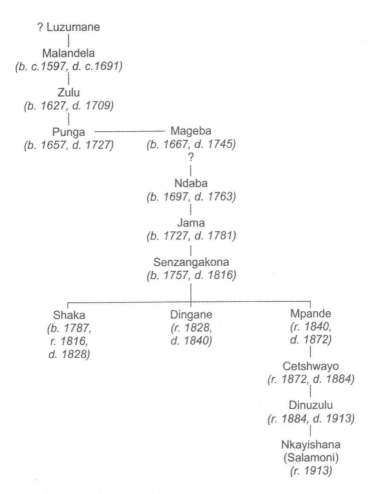

Shaka's family genealogy, according to A. T. Bryant.

The Qwabe who lived between the Tugela and Mhlatuze rivers dug themselves in and subsumed the smaller tribes around them; first the Thuli followed by the Cele were pushed across the Tugela into the coastal area and midlands of what is today the province of KwaZulu-Natal. North of the Tugela it was the Ndwandwe under their chief, Zwide, who dominated.

Under Dingiswayo's direction Shaka focused his attention on subjugating the minor tribes near him. As these tribes *khonza*'d, Shaka turned his attention to the tribes between the White and Black Mfolozi rivers, the Mpanza, the Sibiya, the Zungu, the Mabaso, the Makhoba and the Buthelezi as well as minor tribes such as the Phisi, the Mthimkhulu, the Qungebe, the Mbuyeni, the Xulu and the Sikhakhane. In most cases merely the sight of Shaka's *impis* was enough to achieve victory. In some cases these tribes had already *khonza*'d to Dingiswayo and probably even to Senzakhona before him. Shaka merely ensured the transference of loyalty to himself as one by one the chiefs *khonza*'d to him. North of the Buthelezi, the Ntshalini proved to be more difficult. Attempts were made to secure their allegiance but without success. Shaka, under Dingiswayo, had killed Khondlo their chief but the Ntshalini remained loyal to Zwide and the Ndwandwe.[3]

The clans began to move west and apply pressure on the amaPondo kingdom more than 190 miles away. Some refugees fled as far as the Eastern Cape where they sought sanctuary with the Xhosa people. They were the remnants of many different clans fleeing the swathe of terror and soon became known as the Mfengu (from the verb *ukumfenguza*, 'to wander about seeking service').[4]

One of the first white settlers, Francis Fynn, describes witnessing "awful scenes"[5] as refugees fled from the path of terror. On a journey from Port Natal to the Mtata river he described seeing at least six thousand "unhappy beings, having scarcely a human appearance, who were scattered over the country, feeding on every description of animal, and driven by their hungry craving in many instances to devour their fellows".[6]

In June of 1817 Dingiswayo and Shaka targeted Chief Matiwane and his people, the Ngwaweni clan, who lived in an area stretching from Ntabankulu inland towards what is today Gauteng up to present-day Wakkerstroom[7] beyond Zwide and well outside the Mtetwa influence. Matiwane was an extremely intelligent chief, physically powerful and possessed with a short, ferocious temper. Little did Shaka and Dingiswayo know that their actions would set off a chain reaction that would dramatically escalate the slaughter and bloodshed. Two leaders, who would themselves become like spinning tops out of control, were Matiwane of the Ngwaweni and Mzilikazi of the Matabele. As Shaka prepared himself for the attack on the Ngwaweni, word reached Matiwane of Shaka's intentions and so he approached his neighbour Mtimkulu of the Hlubi to guard the clan's cattle in the mountains until the fighting was over. Mtimkulu agreed. The battle was inconclusive as most of the Ngwaweni fled. Shaka was disappointed that Dingiswayo did not follow through and crush Matiwane. When Matiwane asked Mtimkulu of the Hlubi for his cattle back, Mtimkulu refused. Before Dingiswayo could act against the Hlubi, Zwide and the Ndwandwe, probably thinking that Matiwane had been weakened by his confrontation with Dingiswayo, attacked Matiwane and his Ngwaweni. Again the Ngwaweni fled before the Ndwandwe. For the first time people were totally and comprehensively deprived of their lands. Prior to this, victory in battle was measured by the number of the enemy killed and the number of cattle recovered from the vanquished. Despite the Hlubi living in a well-protected mountainous region having being forced off their own lands by Zwide and the

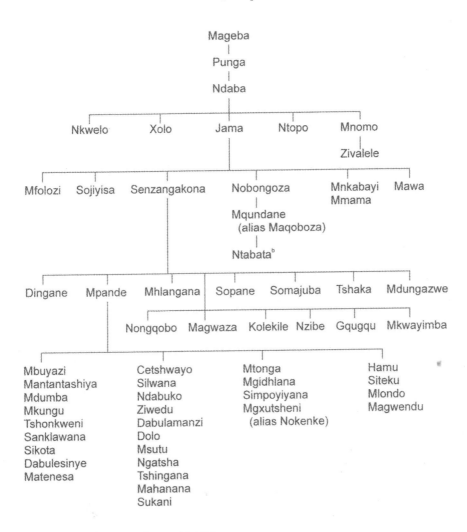

Shaka's family genealogy, according to Mgidhlana.

Ndwandwe, Matiwane, having little option as to where to take his people, decided to attack the Hlubi capital to recover his cattle and to loot and plunder whatever he could. From Ncome river to the source of the Mzinyati river lay the scattered kraals of the Hlubi. With hand-picked warriors Matiwane surrounded Mtimkulu's Great Place, near the inGcuba stream, one night. In the early hours of morning the Ngwaweni warriors stormed the Great Place and hurled every man women and child to their death, including Mtimkulu. All major Hlubi kraals that stood in Matiwane's path were completely destroyed in a series of ferocious attacks. He recovered all his stolen cattle, forcing the remnants of the Hlubi, hotly pursued by his Ngwaweni warriors,

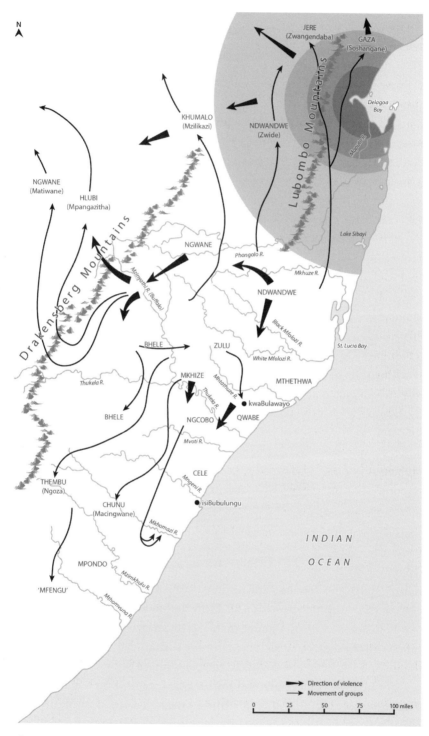

The migrations and conflicts of 1821–24.

to flee across the Drakensberg mountains, where, after reforming and consolidating, they descended on the unsuspecting Sotho clans beyond. This domino effect changed the face of the country.[8] One of the first of the Sotho clans attacked by the Hlubi was the baTlokwa led by a female chief named Mantatisi.[9]

Matiwane forded the Mzinyati river and skirted the eastern flank of the Drakensberg mountains in search of a suitable place to put down roots for his Ngwaweni people. On his way there he entered the lands of the amaBele in the country between the Klip and Sundays rivers. Seeing them as allies of the Hlubi, Matiwane attacked without mercy, burning huts and crops and butchering men, women and children in his path. After crossing the upper Tugela in 1818 he settled his people in a triangle formed by the Tugela and the Drakensberg. For four years Matiwane and his Ngwaweni people lived in relative peace, until in 1822 Shaka's army marched on him. Rather than fight the mighty Zulu, Matiwane gathered his people about him and fled, leaving his cattle and whatever could not be carried as prize to the approaching Zulus. Being forced to flee with his followers over the Drakensberg, Matiwane was unable to establish a kraal economy in time, so, as with the Hlubi, who had also been displaced, he raided and pillaged cattle and crops from the Sotho clans, who in turn were displaced and forced to pillage from their neighbours, who, to survive, were then forced to attack their neighbours and so the domino effect played out.

In 1817 in KwaZulu-Natal the rampant Dingiswayo and Shaka clashed with Zwide and the Ndwandwe. In the first encounter neither side was able to dominate the other in battle, so, unable to defeat Dingiswayo by military means, Zwide decided to use witchcraft. Acknowledging Dingiswayo as a formidable opponent, he sent two of his daughters to court Dingiswayo. He gave each a snuff box and instructed them that when having intercourse with Dingiswayo they should, when he ejaculated, gather some of his semen into the snuff box. There was great jubilation when the young women arrived at the kraal of Dingiswayo, as they had come to marry him. A few days later, after intercourse with Dingiswayo, the two sisters had achieved their goal and with a snuff box containing Dingiswayo's semen, fled back home. When handed the snuff box, Zwide shouted, "Now I have overcome him!" He then mixed *muti*, medicine, to put Dingiswayo in his power, it being common belief that if someone gained access to his enemy's body fluids, he (the enemy) would become weak and vulnerable, leading to his defeat

Without warning, Dingiswayo commanded his warriors to prepare for war against Zwide. So sudden was the order that many of his *indunas* remonstrated with him for the hastiness of his actions. It may well have been that Dingiswayo realized that he had been tricked by Zwide's daughters. So quickly did Dingiswayo act that he did not wait to call up his regular regiments but acted impulsively with only those regiments immediately to hand.[10] During the battle that followed, Shaka, commanding one wing of the army, deliberately held his *impi* back, weakening the attacking forces of Dingiswayo.[11] Knowing Dingiswayo's habits, Shaka knew that he would run ahead of his warriors and thus unprotected would make himself vulnerable to an attack on his person. After the unsuspecting Dingiswayo had run ahead of his regiments, Shaka secretly sent a message to the enemy informing them of Dingiswayo's position. During the battle, the Mtetwa, being far too weak in numbers were surrounded by Zwide's army and took Dingiswayo prisoner. Initially Zwide was content to let Dingiswayo live but was persuaded by his mother to execute Dingiswayo: "If you don't kill him, he will kill you." Dingiswayo was kept alive for three days before being spreadeagled face upward on the ground with stakes driven through his hands and feet, and killed by the trampling of cattle over him. Leaderless the Mtetwa were crushed by the Ndwandwe. As was the custom some of the vanquished joined the ranks of the Ndwandwe and others drifted back to their kraals.

But again Shaka's plans were foiled. Instead of the Mtetwe acknowledging Shaka as their chief, they selected Dingiswayo's brother, Mondiso, as the chief. However, many of the vassal tribes of the Mtetwa refused to accept Mondiso. Shaka rallied his own supporters and, capitalizing on the varying loyalties of the vassal tribes conquered by Dingiswayo, plotted against Mondiso. He staged a dancing competition, in which he invited Mondiso to participate. Shaka led the proceedings and performed first. When it was Mondiso's turn Shaka's warriors, hidden in the nearby bushes, leaped from their cover and attacked Mondiso and his followers, slaughtering them all.[12] Shaka was now undisputed king of the Zulu and set about unifying all the different factions under his overall auhority. Any tribe that resisted was annihilated absolutely down to the smallest baby.[13]

3. MATIWANE'S PATH OF TERROR

Matiwane's first encounters with the Sotho were with the baTlokwa tribe—near today's town of Harrismith—who when displaced, under their female chief Mantatisi began a wave of terror in turn. Matiwane then attacked and plundered the baMolibeli under Chief Ratsotsane, ransacking their granaries; then the maPhutung, stealing their cattle, before attacking and burning the homes of the baTsweneng under Khiba. In about 1823 Matiwane attacked Moshesh (Mshweshwe) at Butabute (now Lesotho) and stole 2,000 head of cattle. Moshesh professed loyalty to his invader and added six more cattle as a sop in the hope that Matiwane would leave him alone. Matiwane made his way to Senyotong and here to his surprise he met up again with the Ngwane and the Hlubi under their leader Mpangazita who had settled in the area.[1]

In 1825 Matiwane and the Ngwaweni attacked the Hlubi. An epic battle ensued which sporadically, and with fluctuating intensity, lasted five days Finally Mpangazita and his forces retreated to a rocky mountain stronghold on the western side of the Caledon river. Here the Ngwaweni tracked him down and killed him, finally resulting in the defeat of the Hlubi and the massacre of the escaping remnants of the Hlubi army by Matiwane and the Ngwaweni.

At that time a number of fugitives under the baTloung Sotho chief Titi had fled to Mpangazita for protection. After Mpangazita's death, they immediately khonza'd to Matiwane who was having none of it. As far as he was concerned they had been the enemy and still were. In revenge for the losses his warriors had suffered in the five-day battle, he ordered the baTloung stripped naked and then driven into a stone-walled cattle kraal together with a herd of bulls and oxen. He posted his warriors around the perimeter of the kraal who then goaded the animals by poking them with their assegais until the animals, frightened and angered and unable to escape, charged and gored the helpless baTloung captives, trampling them underhoof to such an extent that after a while of chaotic frenzy, screams of pain and anguish from animals and man alike, there was very little left of the baTloung, other than Titi, their leader, who managed somehow to escape.

Matiwane then turned his attention to attacking the baTsweneng under Chief Khiba across the Orange river and exterminated the clan outright.[2]

Matiwane then attempted to raid the Thembu ruled by Ngubencuka in the area of modern-day Barkly East to build up his cattle reserves. His army returned emptyhanded and many of the warriors had died from a mysterious disease, which had depleted their ranks. Matiwane turned his attention to Moshesh who had established

The classic Zulu warrior. (Craig Bone)

himself in a practically impregnable mountain stronghold, Thaba Bosiu (Mountain of the Night), not far from where Maseru stands today. News of Matiwane's powers as a great and fearsome leader soon spread across the land and was heard by Moshesh who was still in the early stages of forging a new nation. When Matiwane's depleted army attacked in broad daylight they were decisively driven back by Moshesh's Sotho army. Aware of his vulnerability should Matiwane choose to attack his mountain stronghold again, Moshesh *khonza*'d to Matiwane and paid him royalties, or protection money, to ensure his people's safety. After a few years of paying his dues, Moshesh hit upon a scheme to end his helplessness. He had heard of the achievements of Shaka and his conquests on the eastern side of the Drakensberg. He sent a gift to Shaka, which he knew would be well received. The gift comprised ostrich, crane and black finch feathers together with otter and jackal skins. As these items were essential to the Zulu regiments as part of their uniforms, the gifts were greatly appreciated.

The following year, when Shaka's messengers arrived to collect what had become an expected tithe, they found the cupboard was bare. Moshesh pointed apologetically in the direction of Matiwane and blamed him for the absence of cattle, the expected gift. Shaka immediately ordered the dispatch of a punitive force to attack Matiwane. The Zulu force crossed the Drakensberg over what is today Van Reenen's pass. They then turned south and crossed the Caledon near present-day Maseru and soon ran into the Ngwane at Likhoele who scattered in the path of the Zulu force west of the Caledon. The Zulus then continued over the Orange river and finally decided to return home. On their way back they again encountered the Ngwane at Kolonyama. The Ngwane fled in panic only to run into the Zulu army again at Ladybrand. The Zulus took all their cattle as booty and returned home, not having encountered Matiwane, the man whom Shaka had set out to attack.

Word reached Matiwane that another raider, Mzilikazi and his Matabele people, were also intent on battle. Deciding that discretion was the better part of valour, Matiwane gathered the remnants of his people together and crossed the Orange river to where Aliwal North is today. From there, on 27 August 1827, he launched a second successful attack on the Thembu at Hangklip mountain (near the town of Queenstown today) where he plundered cattle and crops before marching his army to the Mtata river where he decided to settle.[3] He finally began to establish a settlement well away from Shaka and the Zulus near Baziya mountain. It was here, on 24 July 1828, that he encountered Major Dundas and his mixed force of Boer and British soldiers. Dundas ordered his troops to open fire on Matiwane and his people, believing them to be a part of the Zulu army which had invaded the Pondos and the Thembus. Matiwane beat a hasty retreat.

A month later, on 26 August 1828, Matiwane's scouts informed him of the approach of a massive force. A mighty army of 1,000 British soldiers and Boers with cannon and accompanied by 18,000 Xhosa warriors contributed by the chiefs Hintsa and Ngubencuka was marching on the Ngwaweni. Clouds of smoke covered the battlefield as the guns roared. Dozens of Ngwaweni fell, struck down by the 'invisible spears' of the army of Colonel Somerset. Time and again the Ngwaweni attempted to charge the vast army and each time hundreds fell dead. Matiwane, witnessing the slaughter of his army, knew the end was at hand and fled for his life, leaving his people to their fate. His path passed Moshesh's stronghold Thabu Bosiu and, hearing of his adversary's plight, Moshesh offered the fleeing Matiwane sanctuary, which Matiwane, homesick for Zululand, declined and continued on his way to throw himself on the mercy of Shaka.

A decade earlier, in 1818, determined to wipe out the Zulu, the Ndwandwe launched several raids against Shaka. Each time Shaka and the Zulu army was able to beat the attackers off. Finally at the battle at Gqokli hill in the valley of the White Mfolozi the Zulu defeated the Ndwandwe in a fiercely fought battle which saw the left wing of each army victorious over the other and in which, at one point, saw Shaka completely surrounded and in danger of capture or death. Five of Zwide's sons were killed that

A reenactment of a traditional Zulu marriage proposal in the Valley of a Thousand Hills, KwaZulu-Natal. (Eric Enfermero)

day by Shaka's warriors.[4] As the Ndwandwe retreated, they burned everything in their path, slaughtering all they came across. This scorched-earth policy denied grazing for the Zulu cattle and Shaka had to fall back to the coastal country to preserve his resources and build up his forces to withstand future attacks by the Ndwandwe.

Shaka's army rapidly grew in size and strength, and became known for greater slaughters than Dingiswayo's, Shaka fast building a reputation for himself of being a cruel and merciless leader. Having commenced his rule in a restrained and measured manner, he had transformed into a ruthless conqueror. To fight or die was his maxim and any enemy unfortunate enough to be captured was put to death. As he invaded the northeast and then southward toward the coast, his army, ever increasing in numbers, demolished any clans who resisted, exterminating all opposition irrespective of age or sex, sparing none. Many were burned to death, their huts set on fire at night; his barbarous methods of torture and execution became legend. In one of his battles against the archenemy, the Ndwandwe under Zwide, some captured elderly Ndwandwe women were seized and brought before Shaka for interrogation. After successfully eliciting the information he sought, he ordered his men to bind the women with straw and matting, which was then set alight. The women, surrounded by flames and screaming from pain and terror, were driven back into the enemy ranks that watched in horror as the walking cremation approached. There are numerous reports of Shaka ordering the removal of one of his subject's eyes from the sockets and not killing his victim but instead allowing him or her to walk around the kraal as a constant reminder to the Zulu people of the power of Shaka.[5]

After the battle of Gqokli hill, Zwide and his Ndwandwe consolidated their position and reorganized themselves on similar lines to those

A Zulu warrior displaying his feathered headdress. (Andrew Hall)

established by the Zulus. They formed themselves into the *amabutho* system of fighting regiments, and adopted life-size shields and stabbing spears. In 1821 the Ndwandwe, led by two generals, Soshangane and Zwagendaba, moved to attack the Zulu. Shaka ordered his troops to retreat in the face of the oncoming army. All Nguni armies provisioned themselves by foraging for food. As Shaka fell back he ordered his warriors to take their herds of cattle and grain stores with them. The Ndwandwe's lines became stretched and they found there was no grain or cattle to forage. Shaka allowed sufficient skirmishing to take place to whet the appetites of the Ndwandwe but no major battle took place. Shaka drew the Ndwandwe further and further from their own borders over some of the most rugged terrain. Eventually, tired and hungry, the Ndwandwe attempted to retreat with Shaka harassing and harrying them like a terrier nipping and biting, mainly under the cover of darkness. Finally as the Ndwandwe struggled to cross the Mhlatuze river Shaka struck, with a planned night attack on the enemy. His troops were instructed that when they encountered anyone in the dark they should utter only once the word '*kisi*' and kill anyone who did not reply with the same word.[6] An eyewitness described the scene:

> The Ndwandwe came down the Gcongco ridge, passed Empandhleni, and reached the Tugela at Ndondondwana. They then turned about, climbed the Madungela, and went towards Maqonga, below the Komo; they went along the Mvuzae towards the Mhlatuze, where they turned about and set up camp. The Zulu watched them. The next day the Zulu approached coming from Shaka at Eshowe ... at dawn the next day the two armies met at Nomveve. Shaka's warriors fought fiercely with the enemy ... the enemy retreated, then broke and fled. The Ndwandwe were utterly defeated. Ndwandwe and Zulu corpses were lying across one another where the armies met.[7]

Soshangane and Zwagendaba gathered the survivors together and fled into Mozambique. Shaka moved to complete the rout by attacking the heartland of the Ndwandwe but Zwide and his followers slipped away and sought refuge in what became the eastern Transvaal. Shaka and his warriors then proceeded to kill those of the Ndwandwe who refused to accept his leadership. He also killed those of his own who in battle had shown fear or acted in a cowardly way:

> On coming back from the campaign ... he said that the cowards should be picked out. The cowards were then separated. After this their left arms were held up, and they were stabbed under the armpit like goats, Shaka saying, "Let them feel the assegai!" They were then stabbed. These men would then be killed as if they were cattle.[8]

Zulu dancers prepare for their dance. (svdmolen)

A Zulu induna. (Xolanene)

At about this time Shaka's half-brother Dingane had been involved in a scandal surrounding a young girl and to save his life fled for protection to the Qwabe. Shaka, having received a consignment of beads from Delagoa Bay, a market he kept open after the death of Dingiswayo, sent a gift of these beads to Phakathwayo, chief of the Qwabe. The beads were returned to Shaka with a message that Shaka had bewitched the beads in an attempt to cause Phakathwayo's death. Delighted at the excuse to commence hostilities and increase his sphere of influence, Shaka called up his warriors and went to war with the Qwabe. He ordered his army to line up on the banks of the Mhlatuze river opposite the Qwabe. The following morning, on seeing the opposite bank arrayed with Zulu warriors in full battledress, Phakathwayo ordered his regiments, the imQula, izinKonde, abaNtungwa, uZungu, and amaToyatoyi, to line up on his bank. The two armies faced off. The Qwabe made the first move by attempting to cross the river. Shaka's warriors repulsed them. Then it was the turn of the Zulus who were beaten back by the Qwabe. A stalemate ensued. Under cover of darkness Shaka ordered his younger troops upstream to find a crossing there. They succeeded and when the sun rose the next morning, to the shock of the Qwabe they found that Shaka's warriors commanded the heights above Phakathwayo's kraal. The Qwabe retreated followed by Shaka's warriors. The retreat turned into a rout. On watching his warriors scurrying to safety, Phakathwayo suffered a severe shock and fell writhing on the ground with convulsions soon to die from fright, while the Qwabe that did not fall to Zulu assegais, scattered and sought refuge in the Entumeni forest nearby.

Shaka, on hearing the news of Phakathwayo's death, feigned shock and apologized for what had happened to Phakathwayo and informed the Qwabe people that he had merely being trying to get an apology out of Phakathwayo.[9]

Shaka now found himself embroiled in a local political battle as to who was to succeed Phakathwayo as chief of the Qwabe. Having no sons, a struggle ensued among Phakathwayo's brothers, Godolozi, Godide, Vukubulawayo and Nqetho. The brothers had already *khonza*'d to Zwide but very soon realized that the Ndwandwe looked down upon the Qwabe and returned to Shaka.

"So you have come back, have you?" said Shaka to Godolozi. "Why did you pass by me? Because you regard me as having murdered your house, and shed blood!" Godolozi agreed that that was the reason. Shaka replied that as there were no sons to Phakathwayo and therefore no natural heir, he would appoint Nqetho as the chief of the Qwabe but of course reporting to Shaka. He then told Godolozi that he and Godide and Vukubulawayo should return to the lands of the Qwabe, take wives and have children. As a mark of respect he presented Godolozi with a headdress made of feathers.[10]

Shaka was now ready to attack his remaining neighbours. Between 1819 and 1824 his warriors cut down their enemies as far north as the Pongola river and south across the Tugela river into Natal. Across the Buffalo river, the Thembu and the Chunu attempted to make a stand against Shaka but he crushed them, ravaged their women, and plundered their livestock. Thousands of homesteads were destroyed and thousands of head of cattle were taken as many of the lesser tribes abandoned their homes and fled.

Shaka at this time had established his home on the White Mfolozi at a homestead called Bulawayo. ('He who has killed'), however he now felt confident enough to establish a new capital. About 1824[11] he moved south and chose a position for his new capital on a high ridge, with spectacular views over the Mhlatuze valley. This was indeed a capital and consisted of more than 1,500 huts with the outer palisade more than two miles in circumference. This was the new Bulawayo, sometimes referred to as Gibixhegu ('Take out the Old Man', a reference to his victory over Zwide and the Ndwandwe).[12]

After defeating his enemies Shaka would not occupy the territories: this would have stretched his human resources too far but instead appointed chiefs from the conquered tribes who had *khonza*'d to him. The quest for land, cattle and power had turned the area into a raging cauldron of violence. In the west the Griqua, who with guns had commenced cattle raiding, threatened the Zulu. In the south their opponents became the Thembu and the Mpondo whom they first attacked in 1824 raiding for cattle.[13] The area of Natal after the ravages of Shaka was almost entirely depopulated.[14]

In 1824 a new element was injected into an already toxic mix. The white man arrived into the area known today as KwaZulu-Natal.

4. THE BRITISH ARRIVE

In May 1824 a party of Englishmen from Cape Town arrived in Natal including twenty-one-year-old Henry Francis Fynn. The small settlement they established they called Port Natal. Fynn, the son of the owner of the British Hotel in Long Street, Cape Town, was part of the advance party of six on the sloop *Julia*. The rest of the party totalling twenty-six under the leadership of thirty-three-year-old, Lieutenant Francis George Farewell, a veteran of the Napoleonic wars, arrived in July with the purpose of establishing trade with the Zulu and of setting up a permanent trading post at Port Natal.* Farewell had negotiated a deal with a Cape Town company, J. R. Thompson & Co., together with Fynn to represent the company and to act as their agents in trading with the Zulu.

By December 1824 the hardships of living on the edge of civilization as they saw it became too great for the majority of the settlers who returned to Cape Town, more interested in a lifestyle in what had become known as 'Little Paris', leaving only six behind: Farewell, Fynn, John Cane, Henry Ogle, Joseph Powell and Thomas Halstead. The following year the six were joined by James Saunders-King, a retired naval officer, his seventeen-year-old assistant, Nathaniel Isaacs, and a nine-year-old boy, Charles Rawden Maclean who soon became known as John Ross. He had been shipwrecked when the brig *The Mary* sank on entering Port Natal. John Ross and all others aboard had survived.

The beautiful countryside which abounded with lush vegetation and abundant game fell outside British control, which at that time extended from Cape Town to the Fish river in the eastern Cape. Both Fynn and Farewell had attempted to persuade the British authorities to annex the region with no positive results. It was therefore up to them to establish contact with the Zulu.

A small settlement was soon established. Very soon Shaka's wave of terror led Zulu refugees to seek protection with the whites at Port Natal, and quite shortly there were more than 6,000 refugees around the port. Strangely, Shaka tacitly gave his consent and did not take offence that the whites were assisting his fleeing subjects.[1]

It was at this time that Farewell and Fynn visited Shaka at Bulawayo. During the festivities which Shaka ordered to impress his guests, and while Shaka was

---

* Natal was named so by the Portuguese naval explorer Vasco da Gama in 1497, when he put into the bay. Natal was proclaimed a Crown colony in 1843, and Port Natal was proclaimed as the Borough of Durban in 1854, becoming the city of Durban, the third most populous South African city and the largest port in Africa.

A contemporary drawing of Port Natal, looking deceptively pastoral.

dancing, a shriek was heard. Shaka had been stabbed. Chaos reigned. Eventually in the pandemonium Fynn found his way to Shaka's hut. After initially being prevented from entering, he found Shaka critically wounded and spitting blood, stabbed by an assegai under the arm. The blade had penetrated his ribs under the left breast but despite the spitting blood it appeared not to have pierced the lungs. Fynn washed the wound with chamomile tea, the only medication he had available, and bound the wound with a linen bandage. Shaka's own *nyanga* (shaman, today known as a traditional healer) attended him as well and attempted to establish whether or not any poison had been used on the blade. As news of the attempt on Shaka's life spread, a crowd gathered outside his kraal and waited to hear news of the king.

As they wailed and ululated in anguish, so did Shaka. He cried the whole night through, expecting the worst. By morning the scene outside his hut was one of total chaos. Distraught followers threw themselves onto the ground in anguish. People howled and sobbed and fought. Then they began to kill each other. Some were killed by the mob for not weeping enough, some were killed for putting spittle in their eyes, some were killed

This sketch was originally titled 'Amaci Kafir Dance—Alfred County, Natal'.

for sitting down. Fortunately medicine organized by Farewell arrived for Fynn to attend to Shaka. Word was received that six other Zulus had been stabbed in the same attack and it was believed that the assassins had been sent by Sikhunyana, king of the Ndwandwe. Sikhunyana had succeeded Zwide who had earlier fled across the Drakensberg with many of his Ndwandwe followers. Two regiments were immediately dispatched to search for the attackers. For four days Shaka lay, while Fynn attended to his wounds. The crowd outside had in the meantime swelled to over 30,000 subjects. Many had been killed for not grieving enough or for having returned home to eat. It was only on the fourth day that a few beasts were slaughtered for food for the masses. On the afternoon of the fifth day, the two regiments returned with the bodies of three men whom they had killed in the bush, claiming they were the perpetrators of the assassination attempt. The bodies were laid on the ground at a distance of a mile from the kraal. Their right ears had been cut off. The crowd of 30,000 then surged towards the bodies, howling for revenge. One by one they struck the bodies several times with a stick, dropping the stick next to the corpses when their anger was spent. Before too long there was nothing left, not even a bloody pulp. The crowd then followed three *indunas*, each holding aloft like a trophy a stick with an ear of a supposed assassin impaled on it. In this manner the crowd surged towards Shaka's kraal. On hearing the news that Shaka was recovering and was out of danger, the mourning and wailing turned into a celebratory party and the tumult subsided.

Farewell joined Fynn at Shaka's kraal. Shaka made a grant of land to Farewell, which extended fifty miles inland and thirty-five miles down the coast including the area of Port Natal.[2]

A force of over 1,000 men led by Sikhunyana was sent to attack the remnants of the Ndwandwe who they believed were responsible for the assassination attempt on Shaka. They returned a few days later having burned down several kraals and taken over 800 head of cattle.

After much ritual Mbekwana made a fiery speech in which he called for revenge against the entire Ndwandwe people. A force of over 7,000 Zulus was assembled and under the command of Benziwana, marched to attack the Ndwandwe. Fynn and Farewell returned to Port Natal.

Zwide had led the main body of the Ndwandwe, together with his followers and remnants of other defeated tribes into what became the eastern Transvaal. In 1825 Zwide died and was succeeded by his son Sikhunyana as king of the Ndwandwe. Sikhunyana, for some unknown reason, was not content to spend his years on the other side the Drakensberg mountains but desired to return to the ancestral lands of

Above left: Lieutenant Francis George Farewell, RN, who led the band of British adventurers to Shaka's kingdom.

Above right: Henry Fynn, the first white man to visit Shaka's court.

The Tugela river, such a pivotal artery in the history of KwaZulu-Natal, seen here near its source in the Drakensberg. (Bougnat87)

the Ndwandwe, now controlled almost totally by Shaka. In May 1826 Somaphunga, Sikhunyana's brother, afraid that he was about to be murdered by Sikhunyana, fled to Shaka for protection. Somaphunga also informed Shaka of Sikhunyana's plans to return and to attack Shaka. On hearing the news Shaka was furious. "Oh! My men. I am going to war. I am making war on Sikhunyana. He has returned, for I drove out his father." Shaka then prepared his army for war. At the same time he sent a message to the whites in Port Natal that they had to join his army in the battle against the Ndwandwe.[3]

The whites on being informed were horrified at the request, but as Shaka had appointed them chiefs of their people in Port Natal, Shaka felt perfectly entitled to call on their services as he would of any other chief who had *khonza*'d to him. Fynn and the others were faced with an enormous dilemma. Gunpowder was scarce, weapons were in short supply and the whites realized that by complying they would be breaking the laws of their own country. They decided to visit Bulawayo and discuss their dilemma with Shaka. Shaka was furious and pointed out that they had little option but to comply. After a musket had been forcibly taken by Zulu warriors from the whites and given to one of the Zulu translators, they realized that it would be better to accept Shaka s orders than to antagonize him further. Finally, when Shaka said that they did not need to actually participate in the battle but to only provide moral support, they agreed.

That night the Zulu *impis* marched out to rendezvous at Nobamba some fifty-two miles distant. Each of the Zulu divisions was to march separately and by different routes to attack the Ndwandwe. According to the diary of Henry Francis Fynn who accompanied the warriors, the total body of men women and boys amounted to 50,000. Food was obtained from abandoned villages whence the Ndwandwe had fled at the approach of the Zulu army. After several days of marching, the Zulus came across the Ndwandwe army who had gathered at the top of a mountain, surrounding their cattle to provide protection and positioned lower down the mountain below their women and children. The more than 40,000 Ndwandwe warriors were sitting and waiting for the Zulu attack.[4]

Shaka's army advanced slowly and cautiously in regiments till within twenty yards of the enemy. The Ndwandwe waited. One of the white settlers fired three shots with his gun at the Ndwandwe. The first two shots were ignored but on the third, a roar came from the Ndwandwe warriors as they charged at the Zulu. For a few minutes there was intense hand-to-hand fighting and then both armies fell back. Each side's losses appeared on par. Again the Ndwandwe charged and this time the hand-to-hand battle continued for a longer period and as the two sides again withdrew, it was clear that the Ndwandwe's losses were far greater than those of the Zulu. Inspired, the Zulus charged again. The ranks of the Ndwandwe began to falter, and then collapsed as the Ndwandwe warriors took flight to a nearby forest, from which they were soon driven out and hacked down by the Zulu who slaughtered men, women and children in equal measure. Shaka had finally conquered his archenemy.

The Tugela river meanders to the sea. (smurfatefrog)

5. MZILIKAZI: THE BLOODIEST OF ALL

The lesser chieftains who submitted to Shaka gained his protection against the raids of the Ndwandwe in return for supplying Shaka with men to strengthen his *amabutho* and satisfy his thirst for land and power. One of the warriors who caught Shaka's eye was a member of the Kumalo clan by the name of Mzilikazi. Mzilikazi, a petty chieftain, was the grandson of Zwide and had fled when Zwide had killed Mzilikazi's father. Shaka recognized many of the qualities in Mzilikazi that he himself possessed: cruelty, cunning and with great leadership qualities. In 1822 he entrusted Mzilikazi to command a minor campaign against Maconi and his tribe, the Ntshingila[1] near the Zulu border. Mzilikazi's booty from the raid exceeded his wildest expectations. So much so that he decided to keep the bulk of the looted cattle for himself. Shaka sent messengers to Mzilikazi's kraal to demand the handover of the cattle. Mzilikazi chopped off the messengers' plumes they so proudly wore on their heads and sent them back to Shaka with their tails between their legs. On their return Shaka immediately sent one of his regiments to intimidate Mzilikazi. When they too returned empty handed it became clear that Mzilikazi had thrown down the gauntlet.

Thus Mzilikazi expected a full-scale attack by the Zulu to recover the cattle and Shaka's honour. To prepare himself he marched his army and cattle up the Kwebezi valley and positioned his warriors on a heavily wooded hill at the source of the river, to await Shaka's attack. When Shaka's warriors arrived they found Mzilikazi impregnably dug in and protected by a natural fortress of trees. They could do nothing. They sat down and waited. Then Nzeni, a disgruntled Kumalo, betrayed Mzilikazi. Nzeni knew the route into Mzilikazi's stronghold and imparted this critical information to Shaka's generals. He then guided the umBelebele regiment along the path to enter Mzilikazi's stronghold from the rear, over the hill where Mzilikazi was least expecting an attack. In the massacre that followed all the elders of the clan were butchered as well as hundreds of women. Mzilikazi gathered together two or three hundred of his younger followers and managed to escape, heading north. The year was 1823 and one of the greatest waves of murder and plunder in the history of southern Africa was launched.

*

In early October 1827, Shaka, together with Fynn, was hunting elephants, some fifty-five miles from Bulawayo, when messengers arrived to inform him that his mother Nandi lay desperately ill. Shaka immediately called off the hunt and set off for Nandi's kraal located some three miles west of the royal homestead, Bulawayo. They arrived at Nandi's kraal, emKindini, at midday on 10 October 1827.[2]

Shaka immediately asked Fynn to examine his mother. When Fynn came out the smoke-filled hut he informed Shaka that Nandi was suffering from dysentery, that her position was hopeless and that he did not expect her to live out the day. Shaka dismissed the regiments who had accompanied him on the hunting trip and who were assembled outside the hut and for two hours sat with several of his *indunas*, not uttering a word as he contemplated.

While in this state of meditation, a messenger announced. "Nandi is dead!"

Shaka immediately arose and after instructing his chiefs to do the same, he entered his dwelling and dressed in full battledress.

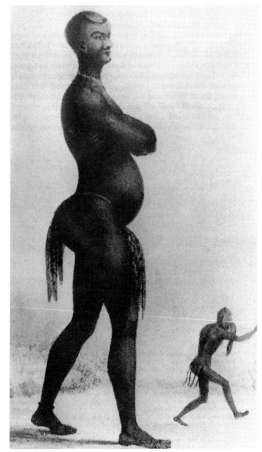

Mzilikazi.

At the announcement of Nandi's death all those present tore from their bodies every bit of ornament that adorned them. Shaka then appeared in front of the hut where Nandi's body lay, surrounded by his chiefs in battledress. He stood silently, watched by a mute, ever-growing crowd, for twenty minutes with his head bowed on his shield as tears ran down his cheeks and dropped onto the ox hide shield. He sighed two or three times and began to scream in anguish, piercing the silence that cloaked the scene. Like a signal, the crowd began to howl and wail their lamentations. As the cries floated across the hills, more and more of Shaka's subjects heard and, as if summoned by the sirens of mythology, they made their way across the hills to join the mourners, the ululations magnifying exponentially.

Throughout the night the raucous lament continued without pause as more and more of Shaka's regiments arrived, adding to the wailing. None dared rest or to even refresh themselves in case their breaks should be mistaken for a lack of feeling or respect. By noon the next day the crowd had grown to more than 60,000 howling men and women. Hundreds began to faint from exhaustion and lack of water and food. Forty oxen were slaughtered as an offering to the spirits, but not for consumption by the 60,000 mourners who were not permitted to drink or eat the whole day as was customary in such cases. The carcasses of the oxen lay on the ground in front of the screaming masses, covered in flies and seemed to develop a life of their own as large black vultures descended upon them and ripped at the flesh, accompanied by hundreds of dogs. The whole force of warriors then surrounded Shaka and sang a war song that must have been a pleasant relief from the hysteria. No sooner had the war song finished than Shaka ordered the execution of several men, chosen at random from the crowd. As these men were clubbed to death, the wailing intensified and then, almost as an act of solidarity, men and women began falling upon their neighbours in the crowd. Those who could no longer force tears were beaten to death as were any near water trying to quench their raging thirst. By afternoon it was estimated that more than 7,000 people lay dead. Anyone who showed any semblance of ceasing to mourn was beaten to death. The bodies along the nearby stream were so numerous that the stream became totally inaccessible and prevented people from crossing. The ground underfoot was sodden with blood, the whole scene such as one might witness in an abattoir as blood and flesh mingled with the dry earth. Such scenes continued throughout the night until ten the following morning when Shaka decreed that refreshments could be taken.

Two days later Nandi was laid to rest in a grave near her hut. She was buried in a sitting position with ten of the best-looking maidens from her kraal buried alive with her. Twelve thousand warriors were set aside to guard her grave for a full year. Shaka's principal *induna*, Ngomane, then made a speech and proposed that as a mark of respect for the great woman the people should make a severe sacrifice: no cultivation of the lands was to take place for a full year, no milk should be drunk but poured onto the ground as the cow was milked, any woman found to be pregnant that year was to be executed along with with her husband. Thus for a year the Zulu nation mourned and while the first two sacrifices were rescinded after a few months, for a year the death sentence was applied to pregnant women and their husbands.[3]

*

In his many discussions with Shaka, Fynn records that Shaka was fascinated by tales of the king of England but saw him, though much respected, as a rival. After hearing of the extent of King George's empire, Shaka realized that he would rather

42

have this important monarch on his side than as an enemy. He decided to use the white Englishmen from Port Natal to cement a relationship between the Zulu and the British, by sending a delegation of Zulus and white settlers to England.

In the white settlement in Port Natal two major factions had developed between Farewell and King. Each attempted to mold his followers into a private army. By the end of 1827 King had won the ear of Shaka and had agreed to lead a delegation to England to establish relations with the British authorities on behalf of Shaka and the Zulu nation. Armed with a treaty drawn up by Shaka promising peaceful relations between the two countries, the party prepared to depart for England. Shaka now had eyes on the Xhosa as his next target and wished to solicit support from the British

Nandi's handmaidens being buried alive with Nandi.

for a military campaign against them. King and his group of Zulus led by Sothobe kaMpangalala and including Mbozamboza and Pikwane (Shaka's most trusted bodyguard) set off by sea from Port Natal on 30 April, 1828 for the next port down the coast, at Algoa Bay, en route to England but due to King being severely ill, the party— King, Hatton, Isaacs and Farewell and his wife—got no further than Port Elizabeth in Algoa Bay.

*

Barely a month after their departure, in May 1828, Shaka put his plan into action and duped Fynn and Ogle to accompany him with some armed Zulu from Port Natal to recover cattle, which he claimed his brother Ngwadi had stolen. Fynn realized when he saw Shaka's 20,000-strong army that this was a full-blown invasion by the Zulu of the amaPondo lands under their chief Faku. Shaka confirmed his intentions to Fynn and added that he would be attacking the amaPondo along the St John's river as well as the Thembu farther inland. At the Umzimkulu river Shaka divided his forces. One

A Zulu maiden. (South African Tourism)

army, under Mdlaka, was to attack the amaPondo on the coast and the other, under Manyundela, was to attack the Thembus on the right flank, inland. Word of the impending Zulu invasion reached the amaPondo and the Thembu. They scattered. The amaPondo ran for the bush as Mdlaka's *impis* swept them toward the Mtata river, burning kraals and grain storage pits as they passed, with little opposition. Simultaneously Manyundela's *impis* clashed with the Thembu and defeated them, but not before Manyundela was killed in the battle.

Just as the amaPondo were reorganizing and regrouping, Mdlaka's *impis* swung back from the Mtata river and attacked again. Again the amaPondo scattered before the might of the Zulu and this time the conquering Zulu took thousands of head of cattle as booty for Shaka. Despite their convincing victories, Shaka ordered the execution of hundreds of warriors for allowing the death in battle of Manyundela. Flushed with success, and much to the dismay of his battle-weary warriors who were anticipating a massive celebratory feast, Shaka then ordered his *impis* to march back to Zululand and to then launch an attack against Shoshangane in the vicinity of Delagoa Bay, a distance of over a thousand miles.

News of the Zulu invasion soon reached the Cape Colony. Major Dundas and a company of imperial troops accompanied by a few mounted Boers set off to attack the invaders. By the time the troops reached the Mtata river, the invaders were gone, the entire region numbed by the Zulu blitzkrieg. Word then reached Dundas that the Zulus were again attacking the Thembus. He set off westward, toward the interior and, on 27 August 1828, sighted a large force of what he took to be Zulu warriors. The imperial troops and the Boers engaged them in battle at Mbholompo and very soon, in the face of overwhelming artillery and firepower, the warriors retreated and fled the field.[4] Dundas believed that he had smashed the Zulu army but he had in fact clashed with and defeated Matiwane's army that had scythed through the country, looting and plundering all in their path.[5]

*

King and his party on a self- built schooner named the *Elizabeth and Susan* (initially christened as the *Shaka*, but soon changed) put in to Algoa Bay on 4 May, 1828. The schooner, built by the carpenter Hatton, had taken three years to put together from the wreckage of Lieutenant King's *Mary* which had been dashed on the rocks at Port Natal. Despite his illness, King still expected to continue with his voyage of diplomatic importance to England, but this was not to be.

The Cape authorities, on hearing the news of King's arrival in Algoa Bay and that he was accompanied by several Zulu *indunas*, including Shaka's lieutenant Sothobe, immediately dispatched one Major Cloete to take charge of the chiefs and act as the representative of the colonial government. Cloete demanded that the chiefs be handed over to him ... for their own protection. King, aware that Fynn might suffer the consequences of Shaka's wrath, grudgingly allowed the chiefs to be taken into custody. For several months Cloete, believeing the *indunas* to be spies, interrogated them at length, leading to great unhappiness among the Zulu prisoners. Having heard stories of the might of the British Empire and expecting to see castles, cities, soldiers and ships, the dusty settlement of Port Elizabeth was a disappointment and destroyed the image of a powerful and influential King George. Added to that, the treatment that they were experiencing at the hands of Major Cloete and their continued detention angered them. One of the Zulu party managed to run away one night to return to Zululand and report to Shaka. Fortunately—for Fynn—his escape was soon noticed and he was brought back to the *Elizabeth and Susan*.

Matters got worse when news reached Major Cloete that the Zulu army was marching to again attack the amaPondo and Thembu. This news reinforced his opinion that Sothobe was a spy and the interrogations intensified. Meanwhile Shaka and his army in fact were marching north to attack Shoshangane in the Delagoa Bay area. Shaka's route was along the Swazi border before arriving in the district where Lydenburg stands today. Near the Steelpoort river, the *impis* replenished their provisions from a local chief, Sekwati, and wound their way round the headwaters

A Zulu *nyanga*, or shaman. This one is a woman. (T. Lindsay Fairclough)

of the Sabi river, then hundreds of miles southeastward to attack Shoshangane in the hill country of Delagoa Bay. Tired, hungry and still grumbling that there had been no break after the invasion of the amaPondo and Thembu, many warriors began to desert. Others, like Shaka's brothers Dingane and Mhlangana, feigned support but secretly began to hatch a plot to kill Shaka.[6]

Unbeknown to Shaka and his army, Shoshangane had an ally far stronger than any *impi*: nature. Dysentery and malaria, exacerbated by hunger, ravaged Shaka's army as thousands died on that long, two-month march. Nevertheless, 20,000 Zulu warriors found Shoshangane well entrenched in the rocks and hills of Delagoa, with his small army of no more than four thousand.

Shaka's *impis*, led by his general Mdlaka, camped within sight of the enemy stronghold and planned to attack in the early morning. Shoshangane had been awaiting their arrival, having being tipped off in advance by a treacherous Zulu *induna*. Under cover of darkness,

Shoshangane's army crept down and attacked the closest unsuspecting regiment as they lay asleep, hacking and butchering the surprised Zulu in the dark. Amidst the panic that ensued in the Zulu ranks, none able to see what was happening, the Zulus fled. As the early morning dawn began to light up the sky, the Zulus regrouped and realizing that they still had vast superiority of numbers, decided to attack Soshangane's stronghold. However, the enemy was gone: satisfied with their success, Soshangane's warriors had dispersed in every direction, leaving the Zulu with no victory and negligible booty. The Zulus, tired and hungry and with a far greater appetite for food than for war, began to wend their way home. En route they plundered from minor tribes in their path, creating a swathe of destruction. After a campaign of over four moths, as the ragged army was approaching the rolling green hills of Zululand, Dingane and Mhlangana slipped away to carry out their plan to remove Shaka.

*

On 2 August, almost four months since the diplomatic mission had arrived in Algoa Bay, HMS *Helicon* sailed into the bay, having been sent from the Cape to transport the party back to Port Natal and bearing gifts for King Shaka. The 'diplomatic mission' arrived back in Port Natal on 17 August. Lieutenant King's health had deteriorated on the return voyage—his liver had packed up—and three weeks later he died. However, the rest of the party including Sotobe set off with the gifts to deliver them to Shaka. The closer they got to Bulawayo, the heavier their dread became. Their mission had been a total disaster and nothing had been accomplished. In addition the gifts sent by the Cape authorities were in the main cheap trinkets unlikely to enthuse Shaka in any way.

On arrival at Shaka's residence, Sothobe piled on the flattery in an attempt to assuage Shaka's anger. While he regaled Shaka with his report of the minor settlement he had visited and that he had only met with "officers of the government", the gifts were laid out at Shaka's feet. Shaka feigned disinterest: the only presents of any value to Shaka were some sheets of copper and a piece of scarlet broadcloth. The rest were beads, mirrors, knives and worthless baubles. Sothobe finished his praise-singing by extolling the virtues of Shaka, comparing him to the insignificant Major Cloete and Algoa Bay. Having now lost all faith in Fynn and the other white settlers, Shaka immediately decided to send another emissary to King George. Examining his gifts which did include a chest containing medicines, he lay on the ground, closed his eyes and went to sleep, in that way expressing his sadness and disappointment with the whole episode.[7]

6. DINGANE: WHO RULES BY FEAR

Since the death of Nandi public opinion had swung against Shaka. It was at the suggestion of two of Dingane's and Mhlangana's twin aunts, Mkabayi and Mmama, who believed that Shaka had murdered their friend Nandi, that the two men plotted Shaka's assassination. Shaka had no friends, as soon became apparent. Mkabayi enlisted Mbhopa's support, one of Shaka's most trusted servants, a man who was in constant contact with Shaka and knew his every movement.

Approaching Dukuza, Dingane and Mhlangana sent a messenger to summon Mbhopa to a meeting. When he arrived the two plotters, through praise and the offer of great wealth, persuaded Mbhopa to assist in the plot. On seeing the return of Dingane and Mhlangana from the Delagoa campaign, Shaka's suspicions were aroused. He began having nightmares. In one of these dreams he saw himself being killed and saw Mbhopa in the service of another king. The women in whom he had confided these visions quickly passed the information on to Mbhopa.

As the sun was setting on 22 September 1828 the plotters put their plan into action. Shaka was hosting some visitors who had arrived to buy crane feathers and monkey, genet and otter skins. Accompanied by the visitors, Shaka strolled to a small kwaNyakamubi kraal, some fifty yards from the Dukuza kraal where his private herd of cattle was kept. As Shaka, wrapped in a skin kaross, watched his cattle returning from the veld, Dingane and Mhlangana arrived to survey the scene. Much to their disappointment the visitors were still with Shaka. A hasty council of war was convened between the two brothers and Mbhopa and it was decided to proceed with the plan anyway. Mbhopa burst into the group, an assegai in one hand and an *nduka* (wooden fighting stick) in the other, and pretended to remonstrate with the attendants who were talking to Shaka. In the mêlée that followed, as Shaka's attendants attempted to calm Mbhopa, a scream came from Shaka as Mhlangana attempted to stab Shaka in the side, but because of the skin kaross the assegai was deflected into Shaka's arm. Dingane then plunged his assegai into Shaka's side.

Shaka turned and saw his two brothers. "Ye children of my father," he wailed, "what is the wrong?" He then attempted to flee, dropping his kaross as he ran. At the entrance to the kraal he stumbled and fell and as he begged for mercy Mbhopa stabbed him through the back. Shaka rolled over in the dust and expired.[1]

The assassins, fearing intervention, immediately killed two nearby *indunas*, one Ingnasconca, an uncle to Nandi, and Nomxamxama. On seeing the violence, those

Dingane and his dog, Makwilana.

in the vicinity ran for cover fearing they would be next. After much persuasion, they were encouraged to return and an ox was killed as a sacrifice to the spirits. An argument between Dingane and Mhlangana then broke out over which brother had the senior rights to drink the gall of the ox. Custom dictated that the gall should be

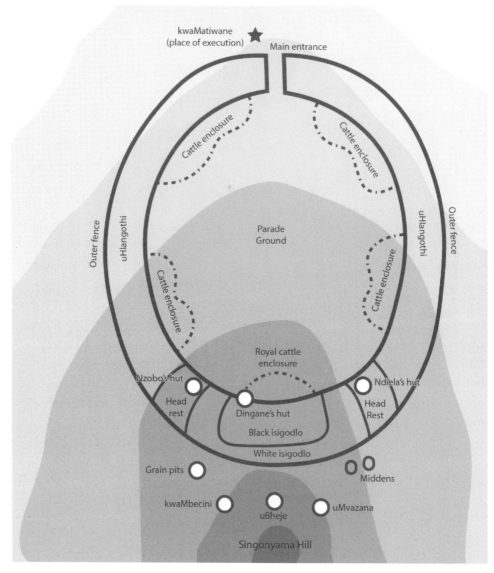

Dingane's royal kraal at uMgungundlovu.

partly drunk, the remainder sprinkled over their bodies and the bladder worn around the arm. Much to Dingane's fury, Mbhopa was confirmed as regent until the return of the army from its ill-fated Delagoa Bay sortie.

That night news of Shaka's death spread throughout the kingdom while his body lay where it had fallen. All his personal possessions were then collected, including several tons of beads, brass, his weapons and shields, plus any item that he had handled. A grave was then dug, Shaka's mat was placed in the grave and the body laid on the mat with his head on a pillow. All his property was placed beside him and the grave then filled with soil. A hut was built over the grave and guards were posted to prevent the entry of anyone into the hut on pain of death.

Mbhopa then assumed the role of head of state until the return of the army. Determined to ensure no further succession claims, he immediately ordered two *impis* to attack Ngwadi, another of Nandi's sons who they feared might throw his hat into the ring as a challenger. Ngwadi had been much liked and respected by Shaka and had ruled over his people with little interference from the king. The one regiment was comprised of the sick, lame and lazy, the 'draft dodgers' who had managed to avoid campaign service plus menial workers and herders[2] rounded up to serve in the newly formed regiment. The other regiment was the Nyosi ('Bees'), which Shaka had formed and which consisted of young, strong warriors. In overall command was Mbhopa himself. Before dealing with Ngwadi, the newly formed regiments were sent on a mission to round up all the royal cattle that had belonged to Shaka in the southern parts of Natal for fear that the amaPondo and Thembu and other tribes, on hearing the news of Shaka's death, might launch their own cattle raids. Meanwhile, while Mbhopa ruled as regent, the two main contenders to the throne, Dingane and Mhlangana, argued and bickered at every opportunity, each determined to establish himself as the heir to Shaka's crown.

Apart from being allowed his semi-autonomy by Shaka, Ngwadi commanded a much-respected army, developed along the same lines as Shaka's own army. Ngwadi had not sent his *impis* on the ill-fated Delagoa Bay adventure and was therefore in a much stronger position than those under Mbhopa.

Realizing this, Mbhopa with 300 men attacked at dawn, hoping to catch Ngwadi off guard. A ferocious battle followed with Ngwadi's warriors showing great bravery in the face of overwhelming odds. Assegais flashed and blood flowed as the two armies clashed in hand-to-hand combat. At the end of the battle only twenty of Mbhopa's men were left standing and every single man of Ngwadi's *impi* had been cut down and killed, including Ngwadi himself, but not before he had killed eight of his attackers; he was finally stabbed in the back by a young Nyosi warrior.[3]

The bickering between Dingane and Mhlangana escalated. Dingane was tipped off that someone had seen Mhlangana sharpening his assegai and immediately, probably correctly, assumed that the assegai was intended to kill him. He dispatched Mbhopa to Mhlangana, the former pretending to favour the latter over Dingane. Mhlangana confirmed his wicked intentions to Mbhopa, who immediately conveyed these to Dingane. Further confirmation was provided of the danger that Dingane was in when one night as Dingane left his hut, an assegai was hurled at him in the

A stylized illustration of Dingane, done by R. Caton Woodville in 1847.

darkness, grazing his side. Dingane knew it was time to remove the last obstacle to his appointment as king of the Zulu, which would happen when the army returned. Mhlangana was invited to attend a meeting with Dingane to discuss affairs of the state, out of public sight near a river. The unsuspecting Mhlangana arrived at the rendezvous unattended. He was immediately attacked by four assassins who wrung his neck and then threw his body over a precipice into the river.

Two weeks later the exhausted army led by Dingane's twenty-four-year-old half-brother Mphande, finally arrived at Dukuza. Dingane was persuaded to spare Mphande as he was considered rather simple and no threat to Dingane's aspirations: a big mistake, as he was much later to discover.

Mdlaka, Shaka's general who had over the years shown great bravery and leadership, was foolish enough to remonstrate with Dingane about the killing of Mhlangana. He was promptly put to death.[4]

Mbhopa, initially rewarded by Dingane, enjoyed a period of grace before he too was eliminated.

Thus, at the age of thirty, Dingane became the unchallenged king of the Zulu.

In 1829 Dingane erected his new capital at uMgungundlovu near the Mkhumbane river, forsaking the old Dukuza site. A Boer, T. Potgieter, subsequently annexed this 6,030-acre site in 1844 with British sanction. The town of Stanger stands there today.[5]

Matiwane, after leaving Moshesh and declining his offer of sanctuary, unaware that Shaka was dead and desperately homesick, returned to Zululand. He discovered Shaka assassinated and Dingane now the ruler. Dingane welcomed Matiwane and accommodated him, together with the remnants of his army, for a short period at a site known as Hlomo Amabuthu, the hill where he usually assembled his warriors before going onto battle. It wasn't long before Dingane summoned Matiwane to a meeting. Matiwane, aware of the vagaries of Dingane, feared for the worst and before departing for the meeting removed his brass armband and gave it to his son Zikali whom he instructed to stay behind.

"Where are your people?" Dingane asked.

"Here they are, all that is left of them," replied Matiwane.

Dingane then ordered the remnants of Matiwane's army to be executed. This was done by each man's head being twisted and his neck broken. It was then Matiwane's turn. His eyes were first gouged out and wooden pegs hammered up his nostrils into his brain. Matiwane's wave of terror was ended.[6]

After some years in exile in Swaziland, Zikali returned to Zululand and gathered together scatterings of the Ngwaweni to form a new clan to be known as aba-kwa-Zikali. When Dingane assumed power the might of Mzilikazi and his abundant

Dingane's spring where his maidens drew water, taken in 2011. (Robin Binckes)

herds were already legend. Added to this was that Mzilikazi had insulted Shaka and the Zulu people. In April 1830 Dingane dispatched the army under the command of his general Uhlele to attack Mzilikazi on the Apies river near present-day Pretoria. Mzilikazi's spies reported the approach of Uhlele's *impis*.[7]

Mzilikazi's available forces were severely diminished as the bulk of his army was ravaging the lands north of the Limpopo. Realizing his vulnerability, he sent messengers to Sikhunyana, the son of Zwide, who occupied the territory adjacent to the Matabele and asked for his assistance. Sikhunyana coolly turned down the request. Mzilikazi was on his own. Mzilikazi marched out to meet the Zulu regiments camped between the source of Mpebane river and the Bekane river, a tributary of the Limpopo. After much posturing by both sides arrayed in battledress, eventually battle was joined. The Matabele eventually gained the upper hand and routed the Zulus. Mzilikazi then retired to his mountain stronghold. The following morning Uhlele arrived on the battlefield, and with the remnants of his *impis* set fire to the

uMgungundlovu today. (Robin Binckes)

abandoned Matabele homes in an attempt to salvage some of his tattered reputation. He then returned home to Dingane, announcing the end of a successful campaign against the Matabele.

Meanwhile the warrior queen Mantatisi led her baTlokwa people on a journey of destruction toward the southwest. In a short period of time she and her hordes had demolished the Bafokeng, the baKwena and the maKhwakhwa and had attacked Moshesh and his fast-growing nation of refugees, including members of the remnants of the Hlubi who had fled the turbulent war zone of KwaZulu-Natal. Moshesh was defeated at the battle of Butabute in what is described as the 'War of the Pots' due to Mantatisi having all her tribal crockery broken in the battle. Mantatisi and her Tlokwa then ran up again against the Hlubi under Mpangazita.

7. MZILIKAZI'S RIVERS OF BLOOD

Mzilikazi and the Kumalo had initially attacked the Nyoka in the Vryheid district after first pleading for sanctuary from an attack by Shaka. However, the chief, himself fearing retaliation from Shaka, refused to allow Mzilikazi passage. So Mzilikazi ordered the execution of the chief and had all his men, women and children murdered. Taking all the Nyoka cattle, the killers continued north. Time and again, through deceit and betrayal, after arriving at a kraal seeking shelter, Mzilikazi and his marauders would attack and kill their hosts, taking their cattle and leaving a path of destruction and death behind them. Frequently the young men of the kraal would be pressganged into joining Mzilikazi's growing army. Theirs became a nomadic existence, moving from conquest to conquest, not planting their own crops but preferring to live off others.

Mzilikazi and his followers eventually reached the district of the upper Olifants river, a major tributary of the Limpopo, where he put down temporary roots and erected a semi-permanent home, which he named ekuPumuleni ('Place of Rest'). It was not long before the rest was ended. A local Phuting chief by the name of Makotoko,* together with his neighbor Sibindi, attempted to attack Mzilikazi. They concealed their joint forces behind a herd of their cattle and drove the herd toward the Kumalo with their warriors concealed in the dust behind the cattle. Mzilikazi saw through the ruse and commanded his warriors to charge the oncoming cattle rattling their assegais against their shields and screaming blood-curdling yells. The cattle panicked, turned and stampeded straight into Makotoko's and Sibindi's warriors. Those not trampled to death soon perished on the assegais of the Kumalo. Makotoko, the architect of the failed scheme, after initially evading Mzilikazi was finally captured and brought before him. He showed no respect for Mzilikazi, referring to him as "the cowardly cur who has fled at the sound of Shaka's voice". Mzilikazi ordered that Makotoko be impaled. Mzilikazi's warriors, some who had only recently been part of Makotoko's own army, fell upon Makotoko and bound him with thongs. He was then dragged by the feet to his place of torture where he was anally impaled and fixed on a perch. For two days he lingered on while the children played around him. His body was used as their target for sharpened sticks. Not a sound escaped from his twitching lips for the two days before he finally died. It was here that Mzilikazi's people were first referred to as amaNdebele.[1]

---

* An eyewitness account by Malida refers to Makotoko as the chief Magodonga.

A dramatic sketch of an Matabele charge.

Based at ekuPumuleni, Mzilikazi and his ever-growing band of followers, some voluntary and others not, raided and attacked every small Sotho clan within their range. The cattle would be stolen as would the crops, the kraals burned to the ground and the women taken as wives. Young men would be sucked into the ranks of the *impis*.

In 1823 Mzilikazi was unsuccessful in defeating the Pedi whom he incorrectly identified as easy prey. They turned out to be far more formidable than Mzilikazi thought and repulsed his attacks on two occasions.

In 1826 the final breakup of the Ndwandwe clan occurred and fleeing men and women sought refuge under the increasingly powerful Kumalo. More numbers were gathered from other groups fleeing Shaka's path. The Sotho named this ever-growing army as *maTebele* ('those who disappear or sink down out of sight behind their immense Zulu war-shield of stout cow hide').[2]

Nature was to force Mzilikazi and his Matabele to move again. For several seasons there had been no rain. Despite Mzilikazi calling in his rain doctors, crops remained parched and dying. When the rain doctors failed to alleviate the drought Mzilikazi had them bound and thrown into the river to drown.

Scouts were sent out to explore for a new homeland and reports brought back spoke of a land of promise. Ensuring that nothing would fall into the hands of possible Zulu pursuers, Mzilikazi ordered the burning of ekuPumuleni. To mark the event, three criminals were tied and bound in the centre of the great kraal and the encircling huts and palisades were set alight as Mzilikazi and his Matabele departed to seek out his Promised Land. Mzilikazi had identified the land occupied by the baKwena between the Magaliesberg mountains and the Limpopo river as his nirvana. Densely forested mountains bisected by sparkling rivers and lush grazing with abundant game made this the ideal place to put down roots. The only problem was that the land was occupied. Hundreds of homesteads built of mud and stone dotted the landscape. Undeterred, the rampaging Matabele descended upon the peaceful baKwena and the slaughter began. A wave of terror followed that swept the peaceful baKwena from the face of the earth. In 1830, when the Matabele numbered more than 70,000, Mzilikazi met the British missionary Robert Moffat. The two became great friends. Despite this friendship, Moffat described him as follows:

> Whenever he captured a town, the terrified inhabitants were driven in a mass to the outskirts, when the parents and all the married women would be slaughtered on the spot. Such as had dared to be brave in the defence of their town, with their wives and children were reserved for a still more terrible death: dry grass saturated with fat was tied around their naked bodies and then set on fire. The youths and girls were loaded as beasts of burden with the spoils of the town and marched off to the homes of the victors. If the town was in an isolated position, the helpless infants were left to perish either of hunger or to be devoured by beasts of prey … Should a suspicion arise that there was a chance that a hapless infant might possibly fall into the hands of one of their friends, they prevented this by collecting them into a fold, and after raising over them a pile of brushwood, applied the flaming torch to it, when the fold, the town and all it contained, so lately a scene of mirth, became a heap of ashes.[4]

Mzilikazi was successful in completely eliminating the baKwena from the area and began to establish his own people in the region. Large kraals were built at various places to house his regiments. The enDinaneni and the enKungwini military bases were built on the upper Apies river, each capable of accommodating 10,000 cattle and a garrison of 1,000 Matabele warriors. Farther south the towns of enTsabuhluku and enHlahlandlela where Mzilikazi himself was later to take up residence were built.

Next, Mzilikazi targeted the Mashona chief, Mgibe, beyond the Limpopo and Mzingwane rivers. Five of his best regiments were sent to plunder Mgibe's

The migration of Mzilikazi's Matabele, 1821–39.

magnificent cattle herds. Four years after being humiliated by the Pedi, Mzilikazi returned in force and attacked the Pedi Great Place at Makhwarane where he slaughtered the inmates and stole all the cattle to add to his fast-growing, substantial herds. Six months later he returned and captured those Pedi who had escaped death on the previous foray. These prisoners were put to work as slaves to cut wood for the building of his enHlahlandlela kraal where timber for forty-five huts and palisades for a fence one mile in circumference had to be cut. After being cut by the Pedi prisoners, the heavy green logs had to be carried from the forests to the building site. No food was given to the prisoners. As soon as one collapsed another immediately replaced him.

Attracted by the word that was quickly spreading throughout southern Africa of Mzilikazi's abundant herds, a rival group of marauders known as the Korana-Hottentot, refugees from the Cape Colony who rampaged near the Orange river decided to attack Mzilikazi. After overrunning a smaller military base, they succeeded in carrying off the greater part of Mzilikazi's herd from the enKungwini kraal. Pursued by regiments of the Matabele, the Koranas, driving their stolen cattle ahead, chanced to meet a large group of fleeing Sotho who had been expelled from their homeland by another minor marauder. The Korana left a small portion of their stolen herd with the starving Sotho but continued on their way with the greater part. It wasn't long before Mzilikazi's warriors came upon the unfortunate Sotho. Recognizing the cattle as Mzilikazi's, they attacked the Sotho and killed more than a thousand of them, while the Koranas safely reached home with the main herd.

In June 1831[5] another group of marauders known as the Griqua (people of mixed blood and refugees from the Cape Colony) under their leader Barend Barends then targeted Mzilikazi. Barends put together a motley army comprised of Griqua, Hottentot and some Tswana. While Mzilikazi's *impis* were occupied both in the north and the south, with only elderly men and boys left behind, Barends's army attacked the undefended Matabele homesteads, burning down their kraals and taking the women and children hostage. This ragtag army then headed for home near the Vaal river after they had gathered up thousands of head of cattle. For three days they travelled without hinder. Lulled into a false sense of security, they slowed their pace and on the third night slaughtered many stolen cattle and feasted. Unaware that the Matabele were following them, they carelessly failed to post any sentries. After an orgy of gluttony, they wrapped their karosses around themselves and slept the sleep of the well fed and content. The band of elderly Matabele crept up on them in the dead of the night and, unchallenged, one by one slit the throats of the Barend Barends's sleeping warriors as they lay. Out of a thousand men only three survived to take the message to Barend Barends at his camp on the Vaal river. Disillusioned, he broke camp and returned to Namaqualand (in present-day Nambia).

Mzilikazi's southern regiments next targeted the Basotho led by Moshesh. In March 1831 the Matabele army was camped in the valley below Thaba Bosiu where Moshesh and his people had settled in their impregnable mountain fortress. For a few days, on the banks of a sparkling stream the Matabele army rested, building up their strength after the long march south, watched carefully the whole time by Moshesh's scouts.

While the Matabele rested in preparation for the battle, the Basotho prepared themselves by strengthening the natural fortifications of Thaba Bosiu. After a few more days the Matabele simultaneously attacked the mountain fortress in two places with astounding force, advancing into the folds of the mountain in close formation. The Basotho appeared to be stunned into inactivity until, suddenly, the advancing warriors heard a tremendous roar. They looked up to see whole sections of the mountain collapsing on them. Great boulders and rocks tumbled and bounced down on them, stones showered down, careening off other rocks and gathering speed in a giant cloud of red dust. As the boulders crashed into the packed ranks of the Matabele, crushing all in their path, showers of assegais and sharpened sticks cut down those who up to that point had been fortunate enough to be left standing. The Matabele retreated. Screaming abuse at the retreating invaders, the chiefs urged their Basotho warriors back into the ravine. Some were seen snatching the warriors' plumes from their heads and stamping them underfoot in a display of contempt for the bravery of the Matabele. The second charge, led by the *indunas* themselves, was equally unsuccessful. Again the Matabele were met by a barrage of rocks and stones, followed by a hail of assegais. Again they retreated, this time for good. They reformed on the banks of the river some way away from Thaba Bosiu.

As they were about to march for home, a Basotho, driving some fat oxen, appeared from the direction of the mountain. He stopped in front of the first rank of warriors and shouted: "My King Moshesh salutes you. Supposing that hunger has brought you to his country, he sends you these cattle that you may eat on your way home."

Having being repulsed by Moshesh's army and feeling that he and the Matabele were still too close to the Zulus for comfort and fearing attacks from more Griqua raiders, Mzilikazi began to cast about for a new settlement in the west. He identified land occupied

Robert Moffat, the Scottish missionary who befriended Mzilikazi.

by the Hurutshe, a Tswana people, under their leader Mokhatla. The place was called Mosega, a fertile basin three or four miles wide surrounded by mountains, which contained the source of the Marico river (another Limpopo tributary on today's Botswanan border). Mzilikazi began clearing a path to the west. Two French missionaries, Pellisseur and Propser Lemue from the Paris Evangelical Missionary Society (PEMS), were working with Mokhatla and his people at the time. They became the first to feel the hot breath of Mzilikazi's ire. Mzilikazi sent a summons to the two Frenchmen. When they appeared he asked, "Give me reasons why you should not be expelled from my country?" Pellisseur and Lemue got the message and very quickly in March 1832, departed to set up a mission station at Litaku. Having removed the missionaries, Mzilikazi and his hordes descended upon the land of the Hurutshe and drove them out into the forests and bush, claiming Mosega for themselves. Mzilikazi established a military base at kwaMkwala, the former PEMS mission station, and chose for himself a site fifty miles north between three conical hills on the Marico river as his capital, at eGabeni (eKapain).

Ever watchful of developments and quick to play the political game, in 1834 Mzilikazi sent his prime minister Mncumbata, accompanied by Dr Smith, a friend of Robert Moffat's, to Cape Town where he swore on the part of Mzilikazi King of the Matabele, to Sir Benjamin D'Urban the governor of the Cape Colony, "to be a faithful friend and ally of the colony, to maintain peace, to protect missionaries and generally to act as a promoter of civilization".

From Mosega Mzilikazi's warriors headed northeast and northwest, ethnic-cleansing all before them. After a few years there was no unconquered tribe between the Orange river in the south and the Zambezi in the north and Lake Ngami in the west (in Botswana) and Portuguese East Africa (Mozambique) in the east. The kraals of the Ngwaketse were burned to the ground, the women and children taken as slaves and wives while the men were butchered. Only one tribe was left unharmed: the Ngwato, spared because Mzilikazi admired their proficiency as ironworkers. In return for an annual tax in metal goods they went untouched and so they too joined the hodge-podge of all the refugees, Zulu and others, who had become the mighty Matabele.[6]

8. ENTER THE BOERS

The arrival of the Europeans and their quest for land added a new dimension to the Mfecane. Their intrusion into southern Africa was akin to prodding an already angry bull in the belly with a red-hot poker. First it was the Portuguese who landed in 1486 but found the reception by the Khoikhoi to be so hostile that in 1507 King Manuel of Portugal issued an edict that no Portuguese ships were

The entrance to the Castle of Good Hope in Cape Town. (martinvl)

to stop off at the Cape but rather to anchor off Mozambique, which was considered less dangerous. Because of the perceived danger the Portuguese lost interest in the southern tip of Africa and ultimately colonized Angola and Mozambique, respectively on the west and east coasts of Africa, leaving the Cape open for the arrival of the Dutch.

After an abortive attempt by the British to experiment with using the Cape as a penal colony, on 3 July 1620 two British naval officers, Commodore Shillinge and Commodore Humphrey Fitzherbert ran up the cross of St George on the rump of Lion's Head, part of Table Mountain, in a ceremony marking the (first) British occupation of the Cape. Some wide-eyed Khoikhoi watched them.

Having, like dogs, 'marked their territory', the British did nothing to further their colonial ambition and it was the Dutch who stole a march on them. In 1648 the Dutch ship *Haarlem* was wrecked on the Cape coast and two years later, when some of the survivors had been rescued by a passing ship and returned to safety in Holland, they

Jan van Riebeeck arrives in Table Bay in April 1652, a painting by Charles Davidson Bell.

Right: Jan van Riebeeck (www.rijksmuseum.nl)

Below: A 1726 view of Cape Town. A number of
Dutch East Indiamen lie at anchor in Table Bay.
(Atlas of Mutual Heritage / Koninklijke Bibliotheek)

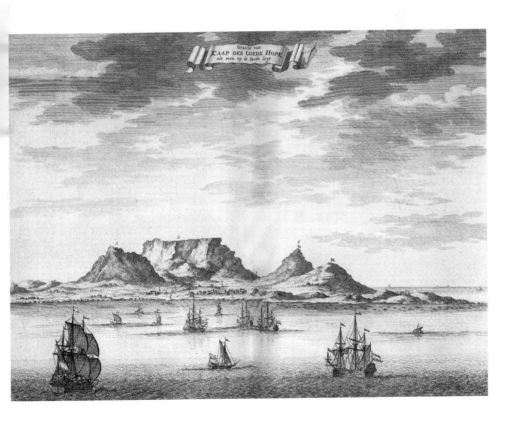

reported back to the all-powerful Dutch East India Company of the suitability of establishing a refreshment station at the Cape.

On the 6 April 1652 three ships of the Dutch East India Company arrived in Table Bay to formally take occupation of the Cape. A disgraced employee of the Dutch East India Company who had been recalled from his position in Southeast Asia for awarding government contracts to members of his family, led the party. His name was Jan van Riebeeck; the Company had given him a second chance to redeem himself. The settlers on the three ships became the first of many Dutch brought out by the Dutch East India Company to supply Dutch ships en route to the East Indies with fresh fruit, vegetables and meat. These *burghers*, or citizens, were the first of the people that came to be known collectively as Boers (lit. farmers) and three centuries later as Afrikaners. The tiny settlement at Table Bay grew rapidly as more and more settlers arrived. Slaves brought by Dutch ships returning to Holland from the East Indies swelled their numbers as did slaves from Malaya, Madagascar and West Africa. Had these settlers remained in what became known as Cape Town things might have been very different. However, it was not to be.

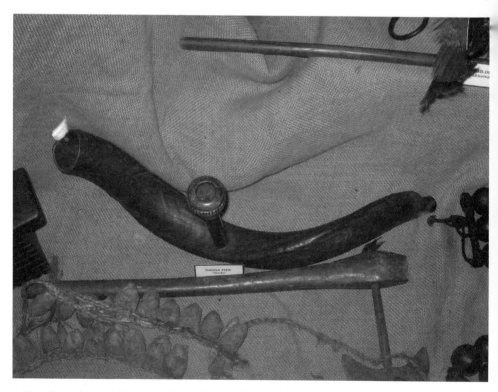

A Boer *dagga* (cannabis) pipe, fashioned from a kudu horn. (Ntonyanine Museum)

Independent-minded and rebelling against authority, these Boers wished to escape the restrictions placed on them by the Dutch East India Company. Hunting parties explored further and further into the interior and in 1688 shipwrecked survivors who had met the Xhosa people in the Transkei area near Port St John's reported favourably of the land they occupied. Groups of Boers began to move away from the Cape, occupying land as they saw fit with little opposition from the Khoikhoi or San. They became known as *trekboers*.

In March 1702 a group of forty-five crossed the Hottentot Holland mountains to explore what lay beyond. Near the Great Fish river they met a group of Xhosa. Much to their astonishment the Xhosa attacked them. The trekboers speedily organized their defences and a fight ensued. One of the Boers was killed while dozens of Xhosa were shot dead. Incensed with what had happened, the Boers murdered the few Xhosa that they had captured and set off back to the Cape, hell bent on inflicting further damage and pain to the Xhosa. Unable, or perhaps unwilling to distinguish Khoikhoi from Xhosa, the trekboers attacked Khoikhoi kraals, shooting and murdering innocent people and burning down their kraals after stealing their livestock and cattle. They returned to the Cape with thousands of head of cattle and sheep. Knowing full well that they were guilty of serious crimes, the men entered into a pact of silence and all signed a document entitled *The Cristian Voyage*, vowing never to betray one another. These men never faced justice.[1]

And so the European trickle gradually turned into a deluge. As the land of the Zulu and the hinterland erupted with the Mfecane, the movement of the trekboers up the southeastern coastline opened a new pressure point until the inevitable happened: they met the Xhosa proper. These trekboers established themselves on farms on the western side of the Great Fish river. On the east bank were the Xhosa. It was all about land and cattle. From 1779 a hundred years of war between the Xhosa and the Cape Colony began. There were nine identifiable conflicts, known at the time as 'kaffir wars' and more modernly as 'frontier wars'.

Two distinct societies had evolved. Cape Town became known as 'Little Paris' where a very sophisticated lifestyle was enjoyed with garden parties, slaves, parades and balls held at the hub of the town, the Castle. Alcohol played a large role in the enjoyment of life and prostitution was rife.

On the frontier it was a very hardy lifestyle. In many cases the trekboers lived in thatched dwellings made from mud and daub. Most slept on clay floors polished with cow dung like the Xhosa. Some dressed in skins and learning from the Khoikhoi and Xhosa covered their bodies with animal fat. Xhosa, Boer and Khoikhoi alike enjoyed the custom of smoking *dagga* (marijuana).

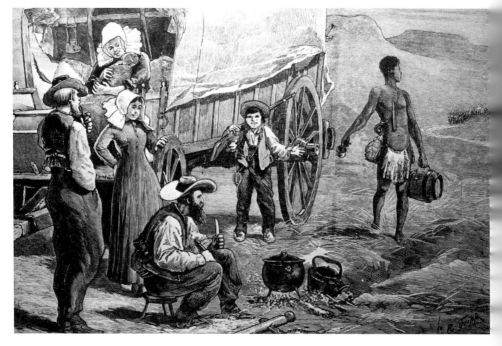

An engraving of outspanned voortrekkers.

In 1795, the British attacked the Dutch in the Cape and took possession of the Cape for England. In 1802 they gave it back to the Dutch and in 1806 they again attacked the Dutch and took possession of the Cape, this time for good, or until 1910. The land up to the Orange river became known as the Cape Colony.

By 1819 the population of the Cape Colony comprised 42,000 Europeans, mainly of Dutch, German and Huguenot descent, 31,700 slaves from the East Indies and Madagascar and 24,450 Khoikhoi referred to as Hottentots. Lord Charles Somerset, the British governor of the colony, planned to strengthen resistance to the Xhosa on the other side the Fish river by establishing a buffer zone between the Xhosa and the Cape. Timing was perfect as the industrial revolution and the end of the Napoleonic wars had created massive unemployment in Britain.

After advertising for settlers, 90,000 applications were received for the proposed hundred-acre farms at £10 apiece. However, the true story was not advertised: a viable farm to sustain a family required 1,200 acres as the farms were located in an area known as Die Zuurveld (the sour grass) where the only successful crop was pineapples, a fact no one knew at the time. Worse, they were to settle the area where war against the Xhosa had been raging for three decades and was still raging. In 1820, 5,000 English settlers were brought out in twenty-one ships. To this day they are known as the 1820 settlers. On arrival, picking their way over the scorching beaches of Algoa Bay with their parasols, they were transported on a ten-day wagon journey to the frontier where their plots had been pegged out among the farms of the trekboers. Over the next few years, after continual crop failures and the Xhosa had worn them down in constant attacks, most of them gave up and sought new lives in the frontier towns such as Graham's Town and Port Elizabeth, and of course back in Cape Town. But despite the deprivations of the frontier, the Boers stayed put.

In 1834 the British grandly announced the abolition of slavery. Most of the slaves in the colony were located in Little Paris, Cape Town. There were few on the frontier. However, the British announced that they would pay compensation of £95 per slave. The kicker, however, was that to receive compensation a claim had to be physically made in England where a 10-shilling-a-slave stamp duty would be charged too.

The sixth frontier war that erupted at the same time was really the straw that broke the camel's back. More than 700 Boers farms were attacked and 456 homesteads burned to the ground. The Boers lost to the Xhosa 114,000 head of cattle, more than

The inhospitable Zuurveld on the frontier of the Eastern Cape, where the English 1820 settlers became an unwilling buffer against the Xhosa. (Courtesy Ralph Goldswain)

A wagon fords a drift, the wagon being more typical of an English wagon than the far larger Boer wagons. (Courtesy Ralph Goldswain)

16,000 sheep and goats and 6,000 horses.[2] To rub salt into the wounds, the European missionaries, intent on converting the local population to Christianity, kept up a constant stream of complaints to their churches back home and to the British authorities, blaming the Boers, in practically every instance, of promoting violence against the Xhosa. Then word reached the Boers that the British had 'miscalculated' and were only going to pay out £74 pounds per slave compensation. The rumblings of discontent grew louder. Spurred on by these events, many began to look to the north to make new lives for themselves, outside of British control. The borders of the Cape Colony extended north to the Orange river and once crossed, the *burghers* would not be subjected to British laws: they would be free and as the trekboer wagons were towed across the Orange on rafts, the Boer women stepping ashore, sobbed, "Free at last, free at last!"

Already by the late 1700s, the land across the Orange on the fringe of the Cape Colony was populated with a sprinkling of runaway slaves, escaped convicts, big-game hunters, mavericks and a handful of Boers who had already recognized that they would prefer a life free from British authority. Lawlessness was rife and gangs coalesced, some even becoming tribes in their own right. One among such was the Griqua

9. THE GREAT TREK BEGINS

The Boers began selling their farms in the Cape Colony, while many simply abandoned them, and packed their wagons for a *groot trek*, a migration of more than 10,000 souls over the next few years.

Their canvas-covered wagons, which became their home, their church and at times their fortress, contained their lifelong possessions. Each wagon carried a ton of freight of which a third was gunpowder, a commodity they could not survive without. Their sheep and cattle were herded alongside. From 1835 these treks, small groups of Boers numbering thirty to forty to a group, of which nearly two-thirds were children under the age of sixteen, began to head into the interior. Prominent leaders began to emerge: Trichardt, van Rensburg, Potgieter, Maritz, Uys, Cilliers and Retief. Much debate took place among these leaders as to where their final destination should be. Some wanted to travel north into the interior toward the Soutpansberg mountains and beyond, across the Limpopo, while others wanted to aim northeast over the soaring Drakensberg mountains, in some places more than 11,000 feet high, into the land of the Zulu. At times arguments were so vitriloic that violence between groups threatened to break out.

The great trek[*] began as a trickle of wagons moving north but very quickly turned into a flood. The different groups under their respective leaders made for the mountain of Thaba 'Nchu as their initial destination, a centralized, pivotal point north of the Orange river, not from the borders of Moshesh's Basotho kingdom. There they rested and consolidated, frequently merging with other groups under stronger leaders.

It was at Thaba 'Nchu that they became aware of ever-increasing numbers of sun-whitened bones that littered the veld. It wasn't long before they realized that they were human bones. They were seeing the effects of the ravages of Mzilikazi, Matiwane, Mantatise and Shaka. At times the wagon wheels crunched ceaselessly over the skeletons, the victims of the Mfecane, as far as the eye could see, through vast areas of rolling grassland without a living soul to be seen for literally miles.

The first of the treks to the north was the combined Trichardt–van Rensburg group that parted after a disagreement and travelled in different directions. Unbeknown

---

* The great trek, saw some 10,000 Boers emigrating from the restrictive Cape Colony. At the same time, in contrast, by 1840, nearly 7 million Americans lived in the trans-Appalachian West. However, the Great Trek came to be the cornerstone of Afrikaans nationalist mythology.

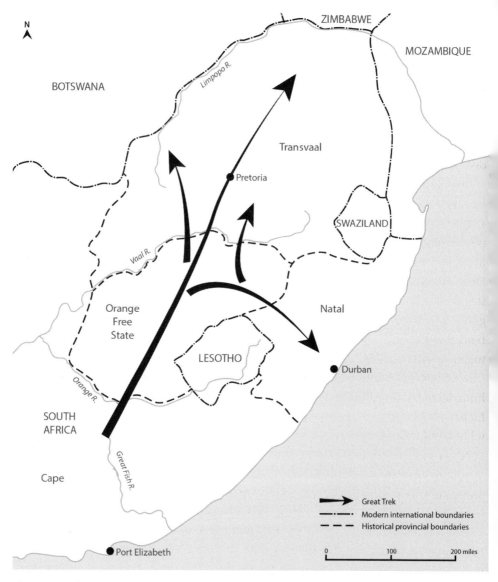

The Great Trek, c. 1836–38.

to Trichardt, the forty-strong party of the van Rensberg trek was massacred in an attack by the Magwamba. Trichardt's party settled in the Soutpansberg where they put down roots by building a church and a library but soon realized that malaria was rife and decided to move again, this time to Portuguese East Africa (Mozambique). Before departing, Trichardt was joined by a scouting party led by Hendrick Potgieter to assess the viability of the area for Potgieter's trek to settle.

Potgieter had left his followers south of the Vaal river with strict instructions that they should remain there until his return, as the feared Matabele under Mzilikazi occupied the territory to the north. After meeting with Trichardt in the Soutpansberg, Potgieter and his small group set off to return to their party waiting at the Vaal. Unbeknown to Potgieter, Matabele scouts had spotted a group of *voortrekkers** who had ignored Potgieter's warnings and had crossed the Vaal river on a hunting expedition. They reported what they had seen to Mzilikazi who gave the order to his warriors. "Kill them." He dispatched an *impi* of 500 warriors to take care of the intruders.

The ill-fated hunting party led by Stephanus Erasmus had split into three groups and were taken completely by surprise by the initial Matabele attack that killed several Boers. Scared and vulnerable, the survivors prepared themselves for battle by positioning their wagons in laager formation—a defensive circle of wagons. The Matabele had divided into two groups. The larger of about 300 attacked the laager. Each charge that the warriors made at the wagons was met with a hail of bullets and the Matabele fell in rows, suffering heavy losses. By mid-afternoon the order was given to retreat. Over half of the 300 warriors lay dead. However, as they left the field of battle, they took with them a thousand head of cattle, several thousand sheep together with captured Boer wagons as well as three children taken hostage.

Meanwhile the smaller *impi* of 200 Matabele had swept onto the camp of another hunting party, near the present town of Parys on the Vaal, and had slaughtered the Liebenberg family, killing six men, two women and six children. Totally unaware of what had happened, as the Potgieter party drew nearer to the Vaal river, Potgieter sent five of his men ahead to fetch fresh horses while he and Sarel Cilliers followed at a more leisurely pace. They then noticed something floating in the water: it was a half-submerged wagon. Alarmed, the men spurred their horses and approached the bank where they found the bodies of the whole Liebenberg family as well as their coloured attendants.† They were the first of a number of bodies that were discovered, Boers who had ignored Potgieter's warnings and had crossed the Vaal. When word of the massacre reached the other members of the Potgieter trek, many turned tail and fled all the way back to Thaba 'Nchu.

Potgieter and his small band joined the bulk of his followers near the Heunings river where he broke the news of the disaster that had befallen the hunting parties. Knowing full well that the Matabele, having tasted success, would follow up with

---

* lit. forward trekkers, or pioneers, it was a term that was only coined after 1880. In Afrikaans culture, it has achieved revered status.

† In the South African context, 'coloured' denotes someone of mixed race, generally a result of union between *burghers* and either Hottentots or slaves. Today the Coloureds are a recognized ethnic grouping.

The striking monument to the battle of Vegkop. (Robin Binckes)

an attack on the wagon train, Potgieter and Cilliers began to prepare for the inevitable battle. Potgieter ordered the men to chain the fifty wagons together in a squared shape and to use thorn bushes to make zarebas to fill every gap between the wagons and between the spokes of the wheels. Two openings were left between the wagons allowing access in and out of the laager. The party consisted of thirty-three men and seven boys old enough to handle a weapon. One of those boys was twelve-year-old Paul Kruger who was to go on to become the president of the South African Republic (the Transvaal) and who would give the British a run for their money in the three-year war known as the Boer War or South African War.

When the raiding party returned to Mzilikazi's base at Mosega, with the *impi* depleted by 150 warriors, despite the large haul of cattle and sheep, Mzilikazi was furious when he received the news that some of the Boers were still alive. He instructed his most respected general, Mkalipi, to select 6,000 warriors and prepare to annihiliate the remainder of the voortrekkers encamped near the Heunings river

The squared-shape laager was positioned at the bottom of a hill that would later be known as Vegkop ('fighting hill'). The ground fell away on the southern side of the square toward a gentle-flowing stream, allowing a good view of the terrain over which the enemy would have to approach.

In early October 1836, while Potgieter was preparing the wagons for the attack that he believed was imminent, Mkalipi led his army of 6,000 out of Mosega toward Heunings river, a distance of 160 miles. Mkalipi's pace was deliberately slow to allow his warriors to conserve their strength for the battle ahead.

On 15 October 1836, with the Matabele not far from Potgieter's wagons, scouts reported back to Mkalipi that they had observed Bataung tribesmen spying on the marching *impis*. They had attempted to capture the spies to prevent them from warning the voortrekkers, but had been unsuccessful. Knowing that the element of surprise was probably lost, Mkalipi increased the pace.

That night voortrekker scouts spotted the Matabele camped only five miles from the laager. Their night fires flickered in the darkness, while Matabele scouts crept up to the wagons and heard the sound of the voortrekkers being led in prayer and hymns by Sarel Cilliers. The sound of the European singing sounded strange to their ears.

As the sun rose the next morning, the Matabele formed into their regiments and sat on their man-sized shields awaiting the commands of their *indunas*. There was a sudden disturbance in the disciplined ranks. A group of Boers had been spotted approaching the seated *impis*. A hiss of derision slid from the lips of the warriors as 12,000 eyes, narrowed in the early light and watched the approach of about thirty white men. When the party was some distance off the riders came to a halt. The Matabele watched curiously while the men huddled together in discussion. Then the Matabele saw three men—Potgieter and Cilliers and a Hottentot translator—detach themselves from the group and ride toward the Matabele. Potgieter and Cilliers carried their Sanna muzzle loaders upright in their hands with a white flag tied to each muzzle. Again, as the two men rode closer, the Matabele expressed their derision: "Sssssssssshhhh" like a snake before striking. The warriors observed. When the three men were within shouting distance Mkalipi stood up expectantly to listen.

"What harm have we done to you? Why have you come to kill and murder us?" shouted the Hottentot translator.

Mkalipi shouted back: "We take orders from one man. Mzilikazi."

It was the trigger for the 6,000 warriors to leap to their feet, shouting, "Mzilikazi! Mzilikazi! Mzilikazi! Mzilikazi!" in a roar that reverberated across the veld.

Then with a shout of *"Bulala amaBoela!"* ("Kill the Boers!") Mkalipi hurled his assegai at the three men. A hail of assegais and stones followed Mkalipi's assegai as the three Boers hunkered down in their saddles, turned and galloped back to the main body of Boers who were watching the unfolding scene with mounting apprehension.

Boer women and children at their wagons. This photo was taken several decades after the Great Trek, but apart from superficial changes in fashion, little had changed.

The Matabele surged forward like a wave of molasses while the Boers dismounted and thirty-five Sannas roared across the veld. Dozens of warriors fell in that first volley. Mkalipi quickly shouted orders to his lieutenants to reform the *impis* into the traditional attack formation, the two horns of the beast that would envelop the enemy and leave the coup de grâce to the head and the chest. But the Boers had remounted and retreated some fifty yards, beyond range of the assegais. Here they again dismounted, took aim at the charging Matabele and fired again. Down went another two dozen warriors as the bullets struck home.

The Boers repeated this tactic sixteen times, killing more than 200 of the Matabele before the wagons hove into view and the Boers galloped into the safety of the laager. Three of the Boers, Floris Visser, Marthinus van der Merwe and Louw du Plessis, were so terrified by what they had seen that they galloped straight past the wagons in a southerly direction, determined to put as much distance as possible between themselves and the Matabele.

Approximately a mile from the wagons the Matabele halted while Mkalipi ordered the army to form into three *impis* of 2,000 men each. They began rounding up the vast herd of Boer cattle grazing in the veld outside the ring of wagons. All the Boers could do was watch in horror as the Matabele began slaughtering the oxen, tearing at the raw flesh with warm blood dripping down their faces. The Boers could hear their laughter as they sharpened their assegais in preparation for battle.

Sarel Cilliers called his people together to pray. It was clear to all the voortrekkers that they were doomed as there was not enough ammunition to kill 6,000 Matabele. Again the sound of singing and praying reached the ears of the Matabele, sounding alien and sinister. When the singing stopped the Matabele saw a white sheet being waved from the laager in what the Boers hoped would be a last chance for peace. But the flag simply fanned the flames of aggression in the breasts of the Matabele and a giant "Sssssssssssshhh" of derision was the only response that the Boers received.

Spurred on by one of Mkalipi's lieutenants and shouting out the name of their leader—"Mziliakaaaaazi!"—the Matabele charged the wagons from all sides. The Boers held their fire as the warriors approached, before, as one, they opened fire. A wall of lead slammed into the leading Matabele and down they tumbled. Smoke

A group of Boer women and children, taken many years after the Great Trek.

billowed from the barrels of the Sannas and screams of pain and anger rent the air. Time and again the Matabele charged. Some managed to reach the wagons but, unable to penetrate the thorny zarebas lodged between the wagons, attempted to climb over. Each time Boer women and children repulsed them by pouring boiling water over them as they clambered down the wagons. Frustrated by their inability to penetrate the laager, the Matabele hurled their assegais like javelins over the wagons as time and time again they charged the wagons and time and time again the lead bullets cut them down. The wall of bodies began to pile higher and higher with each abortive charge. After what seemed like an age, the Matabele began to withdraw while the Boers held their fire to conserve their ammunition.

In frustration Mkalipi shouted at the Boers. "Come out from behind your houses on wheels and fight us like men."

"Come on! Attack us again, you old women with blunt teeth," Potgieter shouted back.

As the Matabele retreated, it appeared the battle was over. Potgieter gazed out at the scene. In their hundreds the bodies of warriors lay grotesquely all about the wagons. Inside the laager 1,137 assegais were counted. Nicolas Potgieter and Nicholas Botha lay dead and fourteen of the men, women and children were wounded, some severely.

The imposing Drakensberg mountains. (Anthony Webb)

Outside the wagons the wall of bodies in the blazing summer sun was already attracting the attention of vultures that circled and wheeled overhead. Suddenly one of the Boers noticed that some of the bodies were sweating. "Dead men don't sweat!" he shouted and fired into piles of corpses. Others opened fire on the 'bodies', causing some to leap up and run for their lives.

The Matabele lost 430 of their warriors to the Boers guns. However, not only had they taken 5,000 head of cattle and 50,000 sheep from the Boers but also a hundred horses. Potgieter and several men gave chase in a vain attempt to recover some of the cattle, following the enormous cloud of red dust that marked the path of the retreating Matabele, but soon gave up to return to their marooned laager.

Unable to move their wagons, the Boers waited in vain for help. Soon their plight became desperate. There was no milk for the babies. There was no meat. There was no water as the nearby rivers were clogged with the rotting corpses of warriors who had staggered there to die or that had been dragged there by the jackals and hyenas. The Boers could not venture out to hunt, ever fearful of another attack. In desperation Potgieter ordered one of his brothers, Hermanus Potgieter, accompanied by Nicholaas Smit, to ride the 150 miles to Thaba 'Nchu to get help.[1]

By the time help finally arrived many of the Boers were at death's door from thirst and hunger. Ironically, help came in the form of Chief Moroka II, head of the Barolong, who had heard of the plight of the stranded voortrekkers. He dispatched food and water and milk for the infants, together with oxen to pull the fifty wagons back to Thaba 'Nchu.

The defeated Matabele returned to Mosega with thousands more head of cattle and sheep to swell the herds of their king, Mzilikazi. Despite the Pyrrhic Boer victory at Vegkop, many of the voortrekkers feared another attack by the Matabele. Each time an alarm was raised the Boers would hurriedly manouevre their wagons into defensive laagers. Persistent rumours of Matabele being spotted in the vicinity of Thaba 'Nchu was enough for some to pack their wagons and head back to the relative safety of the Cape Colony.

10. DEFEAT OF THE MATABELE

As 1836 drew to a close, Potgieter, as one of the principal voortrekker leaders, realized that until the Matabele were totally defeated a peaceful life for the voortrekkers was impossible. He decided to attack Mzilikazi at Mosega. Meanwhile, Mzilikazi had heard that a Barolong chief, Matlaba, who had served under him some time before, had volunteered his services to Potgieter as a guide. Mzilikazi realized that an attack was imminent, left Mosega and travelled to eKapain fifty miles north.

Potgieter, unaware that his main target had flown the nest, assembled a commando of 107 men, supplemented by forty Griqua led by their chief Pieter Davids, some Korana tribesmen and sixty of Chief Sikonyela's Tlokwa warriors, all equally intent on removing the threat of Mzilikazi once and for all. To get them to participate though, Potgieter had had to offer a significant share in the anticipated booty that would result from the defeat of the Matabele. Before departing for Mosega word reached Potgieter from his scouts that Mzilikazi had fled to eKapain. Potgieter decided to press on anyway with the attack.

The Matabele at Mosega should have had plenty of warning of the advance of Potgieter's small force as their progress through the ravaged veld was slow—walking pace—as the mounted voortrekkers had to travel at the same speed as the Tlokwa and Korana on foot.

On 16 January 1837, Potgieter's commando arrived in the vicinity of Mosega and camped in the nearby mountains. Probably because of the absence of Mzilikazi and of his general Mkalipe, the Matabele at Mosega were completely unaware of the impending attack and had not posted sentries. Potgieter's scouts reported this back to him and as the sun rose the next morning Potgieter led off the attack on the unsuspecting Matabele, creeping past the small mission station where a few European missionaries had been allowed to live among the Matabele. Potgieter opened fire at the huts and a deafening volley smashed into the sleeping Matabele. The warriors leaped to their feet, grabbed their shields and assegais and attempted to fight back, but were no match for the guns of the Boers. One Matabele later told his story:

But how could we fight with witches? Our impis went out to face them, but while they were yet a long way off—four times farther than our spears could reach— we saw the smoke, the thunder clapped, and something whistled through the air, while often without warning, while he was yet speaking, one of us would fall and die, with only a little hole to show what had killed him. That day we all believed, and I among them, that the white men were *abatagati* [witches]."[1]

A Matabele brave in full regalia.

The voortrekkers clash with the Matabele, a dramatic portrayal. (Ian Duncan Colvin)

Many turned to flee but were pursued by the mounted Boers and were shot down as they ran. Then the Boers began to set fire to the huts. Soon choking, thick blue smoke enveloped the entire settlement as the huts crackled and burned. The bodies of hundreds of men, women and children lay among the conflagration. Some of the fleeing Matabele stopped at the banks of a nearby river and turned to face the pursuing Boers. More and more warriors soon joined them, all intent on making a stand, but the Boers opened fire before coming into range of the assegais and the warriors were cut to pieces by the Boer Sannas.

Potgieter ordered the gates of the cattle kraal opened and 7,000 head of cattle streamed out, soon to be rounded up and driven back to Thaba 'Nchu. The main force of Boers made their way back to Thaba 'Nchu, leaving a commando of twenty-one men under Hermanus Steyn to burn down any huts still standing and a commando of twenty-five under the leadership of Sarel Cilliers to pursue the fleeing Matabele. Cilliers's scouts riding ahead soon returned with the alarming news that a full *impi* of Matabele was waiting on a hillock ahead to ambush the Boers. When in sight of the Matabele Cilliers ordered his outnumbered Boers to dismount and form a laager with their horses as a paltry form of protection.[2] Mystified by the strange tactics of the Boers and believing that the witches were brewing further magic, the *nyangas** panicked and shouted to the men to flee. The astounded Boers watched as hundreds of warriors threw their shields and assegais aside and sprinted off. That was the end of the battle in which the Matabele lost between 300 and 500 warriors while the voortrekker commando lost two of their Rolong warriors. It was a significant defeat for the Matabele, but they were not yet broken.

Six months later another enemy sought revenge against Mzilikazi. This time it was a Zulu army sent by Dingane. The Zulus arrived at Mosega only to find the charred remains of the town that had been destroyed by the Boers. The surviving Matabele had fled to an area east of eKapain near the Pilansberg mountains. Led by Nhlanganiso, a Matabele deserter as a guide, the Zulu followed their tracks and then split into two groups. The one group tracked the Matabele and attacked two of their villages, killing all the occupants. Mzilikazi himself led his warriors into battle against the Zulu. The fighting was furious and intense as the Zulu warriors hiding behind the huts, ambushed the advancing Matabele who turned and fled. Some distance away the Matabele, spurred on by Mzilikazi, rallied and regrouped in some thick bush. As the pursuing Zulu came into the killing zone, the Matabele struck and though outnumbered by the Zulu, managed to turn the tide. Although the Zulu fled, again the outcome was inconclusive. The Matabele had lost many of their warriors, as had the Zulu. Both claimed victory.[3] While the fighting raged, the other section of the Zulu army rounded up thousands of head of Matabele cattle and sheep that the Boers had not taken. The two sections then linked up and began the journey back to Zululand pursued by the

---

* Previously known as a (politically incorrect) witchdoctor, but encompassing a range of roles and titles: shaman, seer, medicine man, tradional healer etc.

Matabele who in a series of skirmishes and running battles managed to recover some of the cattle. However, when the Zulu *impis* finally returned to Dingane in September they were able to present him with the largest booty of his reign to date.[4]

Mzilikazi had become the regional public enemy number one. A few months later an army made up of Griqua, Korana and Tswana attacked the Matabele and recovered thousands of head of cattle after killing many of the Matabele.[5]

During this time Mzilikazi had frequent discussions with the missionary Robert Moffat with whom he had become very friendly. Moffat repeatedly advised Mzilikazi to move his people north across the Limpopo and to start a new life there beyond the reach of the Boers. His advice to Mzilikazi was to avoid confrontation with the Boers at all costs.[6]

On 14 October 1837, Hendrik Potgieter accompanied by Piet Uys and 330 Boers and about fifty warriors from the Barolong tribe plus sundry coloured attendants departed for the final battle with Mzilikazi. Near the ruins of Mosega, the two leaders, Potgieter and Uys, held a council of war with their lieutenants and the two Barolong chiefs, Matlabe and Mongala, who informed them that it would be necessary to first attack the Matabele town of Mezeg before taking on the main target of eKapain. In the early morning light the Boers and their Barolong allies crept up to the village of Mezeg where again the Matabele were caught leaderless and asleep. Making sure that they were beyond range of the Matabele assegais, the Boers opened fire on the sleeping warriors. Rudely awaken, the Matabele turned and fled, trying desperately to escape the hail of death. Women and children screamed in terror as they sought escape. The Barolong warriors pursued the fleeing Matabele and then set fire to the huts. A rain of bullets cut down any Matabele who put up a fight. The air was filled with the sound of drums as the Matabele beat out a desperate warning of imminent attack to Mzilikazi at eKapain. Soon the burning huts marked a ribbon of fire stretching from Mezeg to eKapain.

Mzilikazi called out his warriors and accompanied by his general Marap, led a counterattack against the voortrekkers at Maaierskraal, ordering his regiments into the 'horns of the beast' formation in an attempt to surround the voortrekkers. But Potgieter instructed his mounted commandos to form a square with the men facing outward to prevent the Matabele from engulfing them. Potgieter then led a mounted charge, firing at isolated groups of Matabele. Gradually the battle shifted north toward eKapain. By 9 November 1837, the Boers had fought and burned their way to eKapain where the Matabele had regrouped in preparation for the final battle.

Having experienced combat against the mounted Boers, Mzilikazi ordered a regiment of warriors to sharpen the horns of their oxen and to ride them at the Boers when they approached. As the voortekkers approached eKapain, they were staggered to see the Matabele riding oxen toward them. They quickly recovered from the surprise and opened fire at the charging beasts and their riders. The roar of the guns and the smell of blood terrified the oxen, causing them to panic and bolt. Snorting and bellowing, they stampeded back into the scattering ranks of the Matabele, who, unable to match the guns of the Boers, turned and fled north, leaving more than a thousand of their number dead at eKapain. In the nine-day battle the Boers had not lost a man but had killed more than 3,000 of Mzilikazi's 20,000 warriors.

On the 12 November 1837 the remnants of the army and all the women and children crossed over the Dwarsberg mountains to seek a new land. Disparate groups of refugees linked up with other groups and slowly the Matabele nation wound its way north, much depleted in number as many of the Sotho-Tswana who had been incorporated into Mzilikazi's fiefdom broke free as did many of the Nguni subjects. The 15,000 or so Matabele made their way across the Limpopo into what is now south-eastern Botswana, onto the lands of the Ngwato, a Tswana-speaking people who had previously been attacked by the Matabele. Not wishing to experience a repeat performance, the Ngwato fled and scattered. The Matabele occupied their lands, harvested their crops and plundered their cattle before moving on, heading north.

Part of the southern African diaspora, warriors of the Angoni, a Zulu sub-clan that clashed with Mzilikazi in 1825, and migrated north of the Zambezi into present-day Zambia, (Alice Werner)

Early in 1838 Mzilikazi split his followers into two equal-sized groups. He took command of the one and headed northwest while his general, Kalipi aka Gundwane Ndiweni, went northeast with many of Mzilikazi's family including the heir apparent, Nkulumane. Kalipi and his party then turned north and by June 1838 had established his people in a settlement northeast of the Matopos Hills (now Matobo Hills in present-day southwestern Zimbabwe) at a site called Bulawayo, after the one in Zululand.

Mzilikazi and his group reached the Makgadikgadi Pan, the vast salt flats of notheastern Botswana, before proceeding northeast across the Zambezi. Here a new and far deadlier enemy than man—the tsetse fly—attacked. According to the missionary Moffat, "The cattle died so rapidly that their carcasses were lying in sight of each other along the course they had taken and where they stopped for the night hundreds were left dead." Mzilikazi then swung southeast and eventually arrived at Kalipi's settlement in the Matopos area. What should have been a joyous reunion was anything but. Having heard rumours that Mzilikazi had been killed, Kalipi had, not unreasonably, installed Nkulumane as king. Clashes between the two groups broke out and blood was spilled. Mzilikazi ordered the execution of the once-loyal Kalipi and all the other ringleaders involved. It is believed that Nkulumane was tied to a tree and strangled, as it was illegal to shed royal blood.[7]

The Matabele were to settle among and subjugate the Karanga, a Shona people who had migrated to this part of Zimbabwe as early as AD 900.[*] On the arrival of the Matabele, some of the Karanga fled while others remained and assimilated, soon adopting Ndebele, the Matabele language. During the 1840s Mzilikazi frequently clashed with the neighbouring Rozwi to the east and with the Ngwato in the southwest. But by 1857, Tohwechipi, the leader of the Rozwi, finally accepted defeat, as did the Ngwato, paying homage to Mzilikazi and accepting that the territory north of the Shashe river was Mzilikazi's kingdom, with its hub a forty-mile radius of Bulawayo.[8]

---

[*] The Shona in southwestern Zimbabwe spoke the Karanga dialect of chiShona, the Karanga being a part of the once-mighty Rozwi empire that controlled the trade routes from southern Zimbabwe and Botswana to the Indian Ocean via the Limpopo basin, the conduit for gold, ivory and slaves to the Arab traders at Inhambane and Sofala. The Rozwi empire was at its zenith between AD 1300 and 1400, its magnificent capital at Great Zimbabwe falling into disrepair apparently after a series of devastating droughts. The Rozwi state was not the first powerful Shona polity to emerge: that honour went to the Mwenemutapa kingdom that replicated similar trade functions farther north, along the Zambezi valley.

11. INTRUSION ONTO THE LAND OF THE ZULU

While Potgieter and Uys were driving the Matabele north, the newly elected governor of the United Laagers of the voortrekkers and head of The Free Province of New Holland in South East Africa, Piet Retief, became the sole leader of the eastward-bound trek, the grandiose coaltion soon collapsing. Retief was making ready to push into KwaZulu-Natal. He and well over a thousand wagons were camped in the foothills of the Drakensberg in preparation for the final move into Zululand. He recognized the fact that he would have to negotiate land from Dingane, the king of the Zulus. In October of 1837, he took a party of sixteen men over the Drakensberg to the small English settlement of Port Natal, before continuing on his journey to uMgungundlovu, the home of Dingane.

As the party topped the Drakensberg and gazed out on the lush vegetation below, they realized they had indeed found the Promised Land. Abundant game of every type dotted the landscape. The grass was thick and lush and fruit trees bowed under the weight of ripening pawpaws (papaya), mangos and bananas.

The Boers arrived at uMgungundlovu as the sun was setting on 5 November 1837. When Retief met with Dingane the next day he and his men were firstly entertained by Zulu warriors dancing and engaging in mock battle, displays of total discipline and precision.

In the discussions that followed Dingane agreed to allocate land to the Boers in return for the recovery of some 500 head of cattle that had been stolen from him by chief Sikonyela and the Tlokwa people. Retief was happy to accept the challenge and he and his party returned to the wagons on the other side of the Drakensberg, the Boers eagerly waiting for news

Piet Retief.

87

The treaty between Retief and Dingane, dated 4 February 1838. It was found ten months later, in a satchel hanging from Retief's corpse.

from Retief. Retief was unaware that Dingane had planned to assassinate him and his men on 8 November, but due to the refusal of one of the chiefs to carry out the assassination, the plan was aborted and Retief and his party had blithely gone on their way, unaware of the plot.

Soon after Christmas of 1837, Retief and a party of sixty men set off to recover the rustled cattle from Sikonyela. Before leaving, Retief issued strict instructions that no wagons should cross the mountains until the cattle had been recovered and returned to Dingane. However, impatient voortrekkers disobeyed Retief and traversed the Drakensberg, settlling in the vast area between the Bushman's and Blaukrans rivers.

Retief finally returned with the rustled cattle to uMgungundlovu on the morning of 3 February 1838. The Boers were immediately escorted into the royal kraal and again entertained with dazzling displays of dancing and mock battles. They in turn displayed their skills of horsemanship and marksmanship to the amazement of Dingane and the Zulus. After the entertainment, the Boers, tired from their long ride, retired to the shade of a euphorbia tree outside the main gate of the kraal. Near the euphorbia stood a tree stump, which, unbeknown to the Boers, was sacred as Dingane's father, chief Senzangakhona, had died under the tree and the hallowed area where the Boers sat was known as kwaNkosinkulu, the 'burial place of kings'.[1] The Boers had committed an unforgivable crime by intruding onto this hallowed ground and had caused great offence to Dingane and the Zulu nation. This caused a wave of resentment and the Zulus seethed. In addition Dingane's scouts had informed him of the encroachment of a thousand voortrekker wagons onto their lands between the Blaukrans and Bushman's rivers without consent of the king. Dingane was also aware that Retief had recovered twelve guns and horses from Sikonyela which he had not handed over to him; instead Retief had auctioned these off to his men. Dingane hid his fury well. Retief suspected nothing.

Retief entered into discussions with Dingane and on 5 February agreement was reached that Dingane would permanently grant land west of the Tugela river up to the Umzimvubu river and northward from the sea to "as far as the land is useful", presumed to be the Drakensberg mountains. That night the Zulus heard the sound of horses been ridden around the perimeter of uMgungundlovu by the Boers who were spying out the land. The next morning the *indunas* informed Dingane that the Boers had actually been spying on the Zulus during the night. After personally inspecting the tracks of the Boers horses, Dingane believed that the Boers planned to attack him. He decided to strike first.

On the morning of the 6 February the Boers entered uMgungundlovu for a farewell drink with Dingane. As they walked to the parade ground to take their leave, a

Above, left and opposite above:
The voortrekker memorial
to Piet Retief and his men,
kwaMatiwane. (Robin Binckes)

Piet Retief played by the actor
Dick Cruikshanks in the 1916 film
The Voortrekkers.

A six-span Boer wagon inspanned.

thirteen-year-old white boy, William Wood, the son of an English trader who could speak fluent Zulu and who had been invited by Dingane to stay at the royal kraal, approached them.

After politely greeting the Boers the boy expressed his concerns: "I do not think all is right. I really think you must be careful and on your guard. I suspect Dingane is up to something and it could well be a plot to kill you."

The Boers disregarded him. In a display of peace and friendship Retief had commanded his men to leave their weapons with two Hottentot servants outside the kraal. They entered the arena unarmed. They were soon surrounded by hundreds of Zulu warriors as they sat in front of Dingane drinking beer. Dingane had already decided to kill the Boers. As the warriors sang and danced in a circle around the sixty Boers, the circle grew tighter and tighter. The Boer dogs were the first to scent danger. They began to growl and snarl, baring their teeth as the Zulus got closer. As the rhythm of the drums escalated and the dancing became more frenetic, Dingane suddenly shouted out: "To me, my soldiers! *Bamba!* [Seize them!]. *Bulalani amatakati!* (Kill the wizards!)" The warriors fell upon the Boers, beating them with women's clubs that were usually used to beat skins for the making of skirts and aprons. They dragged the terrified Boers to kwaMatiwane, the hill of execution, where they were beaten and stabbed to death. The last to die was Retief, who was forced to witness the death of his young son. All sixty Boers died. As far as the Zulus were concerned they were executed as common criminals for their intrusion onto hallowed ground, for coming onto the land of the Zulus without consent and for spying. Finally Dingane knew that at some stage there would be conflict and preferred to choose the moment himself. These too were the people who with their guns had defeated the Matabele, something that Dingane had been unable to achieve. The Boers had to die.

12. WEENEN AND ITALENI

Dingane then called his *indunas* together and briefed them on their final mission: to attack the wagons that had crossed the mountains and had settled on his land without his consent and to eliminate the Boers once and for all. A Zulu army of close to 20,000 warriors streamed out of uMgungundlovu toward the wagons between the Bushman's and Blaukrans rivers. By 15 February 1838 the Zulu army had reached a point a few miles from the first of the outlying wagons of the unsuspecting Boers waiting for the return of Retief and his men. Not anticipating trouble, the wagons were scattered over a large area. Under the cover of darkness, near midnight on the 16 February, the Zulu *impis* began to take up positions near the farthest outlying wagons, which belonged to the Liebenbergs (an ill-fated name). When all the regiments were in position they covered a front of twenty miles. Then they charged, slashing and stabbing with their assegais at all in their path. They set fire to the wagons, overrunning the desperate voortrekkers. The sounds of Boer gunshots from the outlying wagons carried back on the night air to the other wagons who mistook these to be those of welcome for the returning Retief party. Women in nightdresses with lanterns aloft streamed from the wagons to welcome their menfolk home only to watch in horror as the sky lit up in the distance, wagons bursting into flames, set alight by the storming *impis*. As the gunshots drew nearer the truth dawned on them: the full might of the Zulu army was bearing down on them.

The next afternoon the victorious Zulus called off their attack, their killing, plundering and looting done, and leaving behind such unimagineable scenes of slaughter and carnage. The voortrekker camps were utterly destroyed. Most of the wagons were husks of smoldering wood and iron, lying on their sides, canvas canopies torn and shredded and floorboards red and slimy with blood. The grass around the wagons was blackened and sticky from the blood of the trekkers while blood-stained feathers from ripped cushions and pillows floated idly in the breeze. Survivors sobbed as they stumbled over broken crockery, children's cribs, toy dolls and household items, looking for loved ones, picking through the bloody debris to collect what they could of stained bed linen and broken furniture. For several days wagons from outlying sites trundled into the area with corpses and bloodied survivors.

The voortrekkers had lost 600 of their people: 110 men, fifty-six women, 185 children and 250 coloured attendants. Ten percent of all Retief's voortrekkers had been killed and one in six of their menfolk. It is still today the biggest defeat suffered by the Boers in their history. The place where the slaughter took place is now known as Weenen ('Place of weeping').

*

On 5 and 6 April, Piet Uys led two Boer commandos, his of 147 men including his twelve-year-old son Dirkie, and the other led by Hendrik Potgieter who commanded 200 men, to attack Dingane and to avenge the killing of their people at Weenen.

At Italeni, not far from uMgungundlovu, the Boers came upon the vanguard of the Zulu army and pursued them, little realizing that they were being drawn into a trap where the main force of 7,000 Zulu warriors was waiting in ambush. Uys unwittingly led his men into the trap and was duly attacked. Potgieter and his men watched from the plain below and despite being begged by some of his men to go to the aid of Uys, Potgieter dithered and would not give the command. Twenty of his followers defied him and rode to join Uys in the desperate fight. Then a warrior stabbed Uys with his assegai. It entered his back near his kidneys and protruded through his chest. Blood poured from the wound, flowing down the side of his horse, Welsier. Uys grabbed the assegai with both hands and pulled the head out of his body. He was bleeding pro-fusely but managed to pull a fellow Boer, whose own horse had fallen, onto his horse up behind him and the two rode in tandem away from the Zulus.

Uys was bleeding badly from his nose and mouth. "Men, I am badly wounded. Leave me behind and save yourselves."

His men refused and gave him some brandy to revive him. Five hundred yards further Uys fainted and fell off his horse. Again his men rallied round and gave him more brandy. After he had fallen off his horse for the fourth time, Uys turned to his men: "Here I must die. You cannot get me to go any further; there is no use in trying to do so. Save yourselves, but fight like brave fellows to the last and hold God before your eyes. Please look after my family."

The men knew Uys was right. The Zulu were closing in on them. They reluctantly turned and began to ride off. When they were fifty yards away Dirkie turned and looked back just as his father raised his fair head for a last look at the departing Boers. It was too much for the boy. He wheeled his horse about. Strong hands tried to hold him back. "I go to be with my father," he cried. As he rode back to where his father lay he shot two Zulu dead. He jumped off his horse and knelt at his father's side, firing at the mass of Zulus surging toward them. Both son and father perished in a hail of assegais.

In the fight that followed the Boers lost a further eight men before, exhausted and defeated, they returned that night to the wagons at Doornkop.

Right: Piet Uys.

Below: Thomas Baines's graphic portrayal of the Zulu massacre of the Boers at Weenen. (Charles Davidson Bell)

As a result of the Boer defeat at Italeni, Potgieter's reputation as a military leader was severely damaged and his commando that had not gone to the aid of the besieged Uys commando became known as the Vlugkommando ('flight commando'). It wasn't long after their return that Potgieter, tired of the whisperings and accusations of cowardice, accompanied by 160 families, left Natal and crossed over the Drakensberg to head back north toward the Limpopo.

The Boers were in a sorry state. They had lost their leader Retief. Uys was dead and Potgieter had departed in disgrace. Only one of the recognized leaders remained and that was Gerhardus Marthinus Maritz and he was extremely ill with dropsy. Disheartened and dejected, many Boers were ready to give up the struggle.[1]

*

When word of Uys's death reached the small settlement of Englishmen at Port Natal, two of the settlers, John Cane and Robert Biggar, put together a ragtag band of fighters, grandiosely named the Grand Army of Natal, to attack the Zulus. It comprised seventeen Englishmen, twenty Hottentots and between 800 and 1,200 Zulu deserters who had fled from Dingane.

Word of the approach of the Grand Army of Natal reached Dingane's half-brother Mphande, who with his two shrewdly experienced generals Nongalaza kaNondela and Madlebe kaMgedeza commanded more than 7,000 warriors.

The Zulus moved south in two columns and using their tactic of the 'horns of the beast', cut off the Grand Army of Natal from the Tugela river and surrounded them. When the Zulus serving in the Grand Army saw that they were surrounded and knowing what fate awaited them, many of them tore off the white calico they were wearing to distinguish themselves from the attacking Zulus. The Zulus attacked in three waves. Each time the Grand Army of Natal managed to drive the Zulus back. When Zulu reinforcements arrived Biggar divided his force into two. However, the Zulus cleverly drove a wedge between the two divisions and surrounded them, cutting them off from each other. Seeing that they were losing the battle, one division attempted to flee to the Tugela river but was cut down by the rampaging Zulus. It became a rout as the Grand Army of Natal turned tail and fled into the bush near the Umhlali river for protection. The Zulus killed more than 530 of the Grand Army of Natal including both Cane and Biggar. Only four Englishmen survived. The strength of the Zulu army was barely dented.

Like a tidal wave on they swept to Port Natal to excise the blemish of the English settlement once and for all. On the 23 April 1838 the fires of the approaching army on the banks of the Umgeni river, only eight miles from the port, could be seen.

Right: A Zulu *nyanga*, or shaman.

Below: A traditional Zulu village, a reenactment. (Jean-Claude Hanon)

A brig in the bay, the *Comet*, fired its cannon in a prearranged signal to the remaining occupants of Port Natal to signal the approach of the Zulu army. Alerted by the shot, the eighteen men and fourteen women with several children hurriedly made their way to the bay and were rowed out to the *Comet* whence they watched in horror the sight of the Zulu army massing on the hill where the Berea mission station stood. The Zulus in the settlement who had sought protection from Dingane—there was no room for them on the *Comet*—ran for cover and attempted to hide in the bush in the hope of escaping Dingane's wrath.

The next day, the Zulus swept into the settlement, burning and looting and killing any renegade Zulus they found in the bushes. For nine days those huddled on the *Comet* watched as the Zulus destroyed everything in sight. Several Zulu women who had been caught were imprisoned in a reed-fenced enclosure. Their hands were tied behind them as they were wrapped in grass mats and set alight. Once the Zulus were sure that all had been destroyed, they headed triumphantly back to uMgungundlovu. The settlers on the *Comet* returned ashore to be met by a scene of wholesale carnage. The *Comet* set sail for Delagoa Bay on 11 May 1838, taking most of the settlers with it and leaving only six of the English who were prepared to start again and rebuild what was to become the city and port of Durban.

Later that same month Maritz attempted to send a punitive army of 350 men against Dingane; however, when it became clear that volunteers from the Cape Colony would not be able to join them due to insufficient horses in the colony, the plans were cancelled.

On the night of 12 August 1838 the Zulus again attacked the voortrekkers in force, near today's Estcourt, in what became known as the battle of Veglaer ('fighting laager'). More than 10,000 warriors under the experienced general Umhlele attacked from the northeast. For three days the battle raged as time after time the Zulus charged voortrekkers' laager. Aided by their two cannon, 'Ou Grietjie' and 'Stelletjie', the Boers managed to drive the Zulus back. Finally Umhlele called his warriors to return to uMgungundlovu, taking with them all the voortrekkers' livestock. Despite having lost several hundred warriors (for the loss of only one Boer), again the Zulu had struck a crucial blow against the voortrekkers.

The voortrekkers were in a sorry state. They had lost their respected leader Piet Retief, they had lost Piet Uys and Hendrik Potgieter had departed in disgrace. Their one remaining leader, Gerrit Maritz, was seriously ill and morale was at its lowest ebb. On 23 September 1838 the gods delivered their final blow: Gerrit Maritz died from dropsy. Leaderless, beset by sickness and disease, as well as poverty, and terrified of further attacks by the Zulu many of the voortrekkers were ready to throw in the towel. When word reached the Cape Colony of their plight attempts were made to rally support for the Natal trekkers.

13. BLOOD RIVER

Late in November 1838 the morale of the voortrekkers was lifted considerably by the arrival of Andries Pretorius accompanied by sixty men, eight wagons and a third cannon, 'Weeskind' (orphan). Pretorius, with considerable experience in native warfare, having fought the Xhosa in the Eastern Cape, was a born leader of men and an excellent strategist and tactician. Sworn in as Chief Commandant on 25 November 1838, he immediately began to make plans to attack Dingane at uMgungundlovu. He selected 460 men, including two Englishmen from Port Natal, to make up his commando. For the first time he introduced a chain of command to a Boer force. He divided his force into five commandos, each under the command of a *veld kommandant*. Appreciating that the Boers fared better against the Zulus from a fortified position rather than in open battle, he arranged for fifty-seven wagons and the three cannon to accompany his force.

On 27 November 1838, the first commando under Daniel Jacobs rode out of the camp, followed a few days later by the others to the preselected rendezvous point on the north bank of the Tugela where they would all link up. Pretorius organized the men into pickets and had the women prepare *veghekke* (fighting hurdles) by covering wooden frames with skins for placing in the gaps between the wagons. The women were also put to work producing *lopers** in preparation for the battle ahead.

He then issued rules and regulations to the men, making it clear that he would not stand for any kind of dissension or disobedience. Demanding total discipline, his mantra was '*Eendracht maak Magt*' ('Unity is Strength') and frequently spoke to the men about the importance of demonstrating valour, manliness, decency, discipline and, above all, exemplary Christian behaviour, as they were, in his words, "God's warriors".

Aware that morale had been at a low ebb when he arrived, Pretorius suggested to Sarel Cilliers that he should come up with a rallying cry to unite the men and give them inspiration in the days ahead, that it should in some way constitute a promise to God in return for His help against the Zulu.

The convoy of wagons with 460 men and sixty Zulu and coloured servants trundled off in the direction of uMgungundlovu on 3 December 1838. Pretorius had the

---

* small cloth bags containing lead shot and sundry bits of metal that when fired from a Sanna would burst approximately twenty yards from the muzzle, dispersing its contents like a shotgun cartridge, not dissimilar to a simple grenade launcher.

wagons travel four abreast, rather than single file, so that the convoy was compact and easier to defend in the event of a Zulu attack en route.

On 4 December, unbeknown to Pretorius and his commando, eighty men of the 72nd Highlanders under Major Charters disembarked the *Helen* in the bay at Port Natal. Charters immediately set up his headquarters in a wooden building adjacent to Maynard's store that belonged to J. Owen Smith. The British had arrived.

On 9 December, after evening prayers, Sarel Cilliers climbed onto the cannon 'Ou Grietjie' to address the men. He had done what Pretorius had asked of him, crafting a rallying cry, or vow:

> My brethren and fellow countrymen, at this moment we stand before the holy God of heaven and earth, to make a promise, if He will be with us and protect us and deliver the enemy into our hands so that we may triumph over him, that we shall observe the day and the date as an anniversary in each year, and a day like the Sabbath, in His honour; and that we shall enjoin our children that they must take part with us in this, for a remembrance even for our posterity; and that if anyone sees a difficulty in this, let him retire from this place. For the honour of His name will be joyfully exalted, and to Him the fame and the honour of victory must be given.[1]

Left and opposite: The battle of Blood river.

On 9 December the wagon convoy was making slow progress because of the thickness of the grass. Pretorius became impatient and commanded his men to burn the grass in front of the wagons to speed things up. He regularly sent his scouts out to try and locate the enemy. The following day one of the scouts galloped back to inform Pretorius that they had found an enemy camp. Pretorius immediately ordered his wagons to manouevre into laager formation near the Umzinyati river in case the Zulu attacked. When no attack materialized Pretorius dispatched a patrol to investigate the strength of the Zulu camp. On their return, they informed Pretorius that they had only found nine Zulu whom they had ambushed and shot.

On 12 December it began to rain—rather an irrititaing *ukukhemezela*, a persistant coastal drizzle—causing some consternation among Pretorius and his men as they realized that if the rain persisted and the Zulus attacked, their gunpowder would likely be damp and therefore ineffective.

Parker, one of the Englishmen from Port Natal, led a patrol that captured a Zulu scout together with some women and children. Pretorius allowed the women and children to go free but instructed one of the women to deliver a message to Dingane at uMgungundlovu. He wrote his name on a piece of white cloth and asked the woman to hand the cloth to Dingane and to tell him that the voortrekkers were coming to join battle with him, and to tell Dingane that if he (Dingane) declared peace and returned the horses and guns he had taken from Retief's party, the voortrekkers would leave him in peace. However, if he did not do so, the Boers would wage war until he was killed, no matter how long it took. The women appreciated Pretorius letting them go free and told him that Dingane would never have freed or pardoned defenceless women. Pretorius told the women that if Dingane sent them or their husbands back with a message they should bear the cloth with his name on, so that his men would know not to harm the messenger.

The rain continued into the following the day, the 13th. Pretorius moved his convoy eastward to be nearer dry firewood, but still the grey *ukukhemezela* continued. Nerves were taut as Boer scouts kept returning with news of increased Zulu activity in the area. Pretorius decided that attack would be the best form of defence.

The next morning, the 14th, he led a commando of 120 men in the incessant drizzle to locate and attack the main Zulu force which he believed to be in the vicinity. Umhlele, the Zulu general, had decided not to wait at uMgungundlovu for the voortrekkers' arrival but rather to come out with the whole 20,000-strong Zulu army and engage the voortrekkers in battle. Zulu scouts were constantly feeding back information to Umhlele of Pretorius's movements. By the end of that day, the 120-man commando returned wet and dispirited to the main camp. They had encountered a small group of Zulu warriors and had killed eight but had not located the Zulu army.

Voortrekker leader Andries Hendrik Potgieter, with his second wife, the widow Van Emmenis.

Early on the morning of 15 December, again in the persistent and irritating drizzle, Pretorius and his convoy crossed over the Buffalo river. Nerves were on edge as scouts kept galloping up to the convoy with news of sightings of Zulu. One group of scouts reported that they had clashed with a Zulu patrol that morning. When news came later that day from two scouts, Johannes Hattingh and Jan Robberts, who had been sent back to report to Pretorius by Veld Kommandant de Lange, that they had discovered the whole Zulu army behind the Nqutu hills about twelve miles southeast of their current position, Pretorius decided to look for a site to set up his laager in preparation for the inevitable battle.

He found what he considered to be the ideal site near the Ncome river, a tributary of the Buffalo river. The terrain in front of him was flat with hills in the distance. When he examined the depth of the river he was delighted to find that opposite where he intended positioning his wagons, the river was too deep for a man to wade across, or even to cross on horseback because of a giant hippo hole that stretched for at least a mile, running north–south along the Ncome. A *donga*, or ravine, some three and a half yards deep and as wide added to his protection as it ran from east to west almost to the bank of the Ncome river. He positioned the wagons in a D or half-moon shape with the base of the D running parallel to the *donga* and a dozen yards from it, and instructed Piet Moolman to prepare the wagons for the attack by positioning the *veghekke* in the spaces between the wagons, also ordering all the wagon wheels to be covered with skins to ensure that no assegais could be thrust through the spokes. For further security Moolman was to ensure that al the *disselbooms** were to be chained together so that the wagons could not be individually manouevred.

Once the wagons were all in position, the straight edge of the D was fifty-five yards long and the radius from the base to the farthest point of the bow of the D was twenty-five yards. This ensured that the men were able to herd the 800 cattle and 700 horses into the protective D. The three cannon were positioned strategically with 'Ou Grietjie' on the northern side, 'Stelletjie' on the eastern side and Pretorius's copper cannon 'Weeskind' on the western side. The positioning of the cannons ensured a strong defense but would also diffuse the loud detonations, thereby reducing the chances of the cattle and horses taking fright and bolting in the middle of the battle. Pretorius then set off in the drizzle with 220 men in the direction of the Nqutu hills to spy out the Zulu army.

Late that afternoon Pretorius's force, on rounding a small hillock, were astonished to see in front of them a seething black mass: more than 18,000 warriors, thirty-six regiments of the Zulu army, were sitting on their life-sized shields silently observing

---

*   the main haulage shaft of a wagon.

Blood river. (Robin Binckes)

the voortrekkers. Cilliers, believing that he could draw the Zulus into the open, suggested to Pretorius that he take fifty men and provoke the Zulus into attacking.
Pretorius felt that as it was near dusk, and still drizzling, it would be foolhardy to
engage the Zulu and so leaving de Lange and a few of his scouts behind, returned to
the laager on the Ncome river. Before sunset the voortrekkers could see the *impis* on
the move, the warriors settling into the Zongonko hills and ridges across the river.
They were soon lost from view as darkness and a thick mist descended on the laager.
Pretorius was keen that the imminent battle should not take place the next day, as
it was the Sabbath; nevertheless, he ordered his men to prepare themselves. In the
thick mist it was difficult to even see one's hand in front of one's face. Pretorius had
*sjamboks** with lanterns affixed placed regularly along the perimeter, some twenty
yards from the wagons and running the full length of all sides of the D. He positioned
eight men between each wagon. Each man was equipped with at least two Sannas, in

---

* a sturdy leather whip.

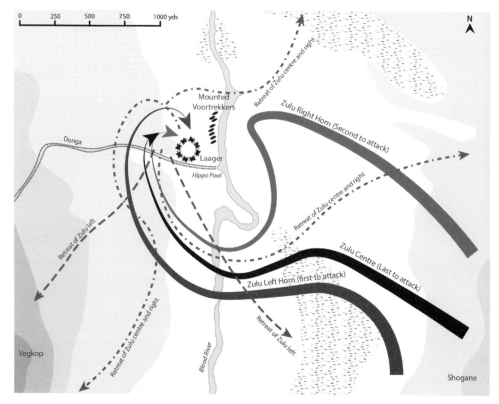

The battle of Blood river.

some cases three, and issued with saucers of gunpowder and a supply of ammunition and *lopers* was placed next to his position.

The cannon were loaded with grapeshot and next to each cannon were piled metal pot legs, sundry bits of iron and stones as ammunition resupply. Each cannon was placed between two back-to-back wagons which could be pushed apart or closed up as the need arose, to ensure that the voortrekkers could exit the laager on horseback during the battle if necessary.

While Pretorius was making his battle preparations, Umhlele led his warriors nearer the laager, positioning the main body of his army on the Zonkonka hill and several *impis* to the east in front of the Khalatu, Nceceni and Teleza hills. Debating with Tambuza, his second-in-command, and his *indunas*, Umhlele questioned the wisdom of attacking that night or drawing the voortrekkers into an ambush. He believed the enemy would have learned from their mistakes following their defeat at Italeni and ruled out an ambush. It was suggested that the Zulu should surround the wagons under the cover of darkness and implement a siege, preventing the voortrekkers from leaving the laager and starving them into submission. Umhlele ruled this out too as he felt that the booty, the voortrekkers' cattle, would also starve in a siege. Instead he decided that under the cover of darkness two-thirds of his force, some 12,000 warriors of the Isihlangu Mnyama ('Black Shields') under the command of Tambuza would quietly make their way downstream and find a point to ford the river before coming back upstream, surrounding the wagons and waiting until first light to launch the attack Umhlele would wait across the river for the initial assault to succeed before he too would ford the river at the same place and then join the battle with his 6,000 warriors of the Isihlangu Mhlope ('White Shields') to finish off the presumably weakened voortrekkers

That night Umhlele's warriors heard the Boers praying and singing psalms. To their ears it sounded like men crying. As they gazed down from the hills the light from the lanterns on the *sjamboks* appeared diffused and eerie, adding to their opinion that they were about to enter into battle against wizards.

A warrior shouted out through the darkness, "Keep on weeping. The sun of tomorrow you will never see set."

Boer cannon at Blood river. (Robin Binckes)

Pretorius instructed his men that they should assume their positions two hours before sunrise to await the probable Zulu attack. It is highly unlikely that any of the men in the laager slept that night. If they dozed they were harshly woken by the sounds of the Zulu war song:

> We journey to war
> Over the hills yonder
> Over the hills where the sun sets,
> To a country we do not know.
> We journey for you, king and father,
> Lion! Elephant! Liberator!
> King of Kings! King of the Zulu! Dingane.
> We greet you!

Late that night Tambuza began to move his men into position and marched them downstream to the crossing point his scouts had earlier identified. As 24,000 feet crossed the river, a noise of rumbling floated up to the voortrekkers as rocks and pebbles displaced in the water rolled under the Zulu feet, creating an eerie roar. By 4 o'clock in the morning Tambuza's 12,000 warriors were in position, sitting on their shields in the darkness in a giant fan formation that stretched from just beyond the ring of *sjambok* lanterns to a depth of more than 150 yards. Tambuza had also ordered an impi to pack the *donga* where the warriors stood shoulder to shoulder waiting for the dawn

As the sky began to lighten, the *impis* heard a cheer from the laager as the voortrekkers realized that the *ukukhemezela* had stopped: their powder would keep dry. The seated Zulus watched as the Boers gazed from out of their wagons in fearful awe at them, the 12,000 warriors surrounding the laager. At the head of the *impis* stood the regimental commanders, fully dressed for battle and watching the antics of the *nyangas* leaping and whirling like dervishes, their cats' tails dangling from their waists like serpents.; around their necks necklaces of yellowed lion and leopard teeth bounced and rattled as they dispensed animal blood over the warriors to protect them from the bullets of the wizards.

Then, as the warriors began to clamber to their feet, a single shot rang out, fired by Pretorius as the signal to the Boers to open fire, immediately followed by a roar as 400 Sannas fired in unison. A wall of lead struck the front row of warriors and down they tumbled. Those not hit leaped to their feet and on the signal of the *icilongo*, the war trumpet, and rallied by the cry of *"Bulala eMaboela!"* from their commanders, the Black Shields charged at the wagons, shouting their war cry of *"Usutu! Usutu! Usutu!"*

The Boer laager at Blood river. (Robin Binckes)

Back came the response, "*Djie! Djie! Djie!*" and as the Zulus bore down on the wagons, a frenzy of fire hit them like a wall. Down they went. On they charged. The sound of the guns became one continuous, deafening roar. The whole area was enveloped in thick, blue smoke, punctuated by the spurts of flame from the barrels of the guns as the Boers fired and fired and fired.

Frustrated at their inability to penetrate the ring of wagons, Tambuza called a halt and the *icilongo* signalled a retreat while the *impis* retired some 300 yards from the laager. When the smoke cleared the Zulu dead and wounded, in their dozens, their hundreds, became apparent. Tambuza held a council of war with his commanders and decided to renew the attack.

The second charge was met with the booming of the cannon and again the roar of the guns became deafening. Some of the warriors were becoming disheartened: losses were too high to sustain as the relentless fire from the Boer guns was preventing the Zulus from reaching the wagons and closing with the enemy.

After a further two hours the guns ceased firing: Tambuza had again signalled a retreat, his impis yet again withdrawing 300 yards. The silence that followed was equally deafening. Again Tambuza consulted with his commanders and this time sent a messenger across the river to Umhlele requesting he commit his Isihlangu Mhlope to battle. While waiting for the response, the Zulus watched as seven mounted Boers galloped toward them, firing from the saddle as they did, before, while still out of assegai range, they wheeled their horses and galloped back to the laager. The incensed Zulus charged again, this time spreading out and making it harder for the voortrekkers to pick out their targets. The tactic worked and far fewer Zulu were killed but the three cannon were still wreaking havoc.

The awaiting Isihlangu Mhlope was in the process of forming up to join the battle and relieve the pressure on the Isihlangu Mnyama when a shout went up: one of Pretorius's cannon had found the range to direct enfilade fire across the river at the Isihlangu Mhlope. The first shell smashed into the earth, sending blood, bones and body parts into the heavens in a shower of gore. Sixty-nine warriors lay dead and dying in and around the crater when the smoke cleared, among them two of Dingane's half-brothers, Zulu princes. Enraged by what they had witnessed, the 6,000 Isihlangu Mhlope rushed to join the battle, many leaping into the deep water

The direction from which the Boers approached at Blood river. (Robin Binckes)

directly opposite the wagons only to be hit by voortrekker bullets, or drown in the heaving mêlée. Valuable time had been wasted as the only way across the river was way downstream.

Unaware that a Zulu victory was close at hand—the Boers were running low on ammunition and powder—the withering voortrekker fire nevertheless continued to take a ruthless toll on the Zulus. Then there were shouts as Bart Pretorius led a hundred men on horseback out of the laager in an attempt to break through the Zulu. Umhlele, who had by now joined the battle, ordered some of his warriors to manouevre themselves behind Pretorius and and cut the Boers off from their laager. Pretorius, realizing what Umhlele was attempting to do, quickly wheeled his horse and led his men back into the laager. Soon after he tried again and again he was denied and returned to the laager. On his third attempt, he was accompanied by 150 Boers. They exited the laager on the the western side and caught the Zulus unaware. Sannas and pistols blazing, they rode straight at the ranks of the Zulu who leaped aside to avoid being crushed underfoot. The mounted Boers, having forced a gap in the ranks of the Zulu, then turned and attacked the Isihlangu Mhlope in the rear. With the Sannas and cannon blazing away from the laager, the Zulu found themselves under attack in a pincer-like movement and the ranks began to break, slowly at first, but as fear and panic took hold, the *impis* turned and fled. Seizing the moment, another commando of mounted Boers came galloping out of the laager, shooting from their saddles at the fleeing warriors, many of whom ran for cover into the reeds along the river but they were shot down in their dozens until the river ran red with their blood. One of the warriors who was there, Lunguza kaMpukane, was to recall many years later:

After we had been repulsed, we ran in all directions. The Boers split up and charged at us. Four came in our direction riding red horses, five in another direction and six in another. They fired at us with their guns. We hid in antbear holes, under antheaps, stuffing our heads into holes even though otherwise exposed. Others hid themselves under the heaps of corpses that were everywhere. Even warriors who were dead were shot again. We stood no chance of escaping.

By the time the battle was done, more than a thousand corpses floated in the Ncome river. The Zulus had lost somewhere between 3,000 and 10,000 of their finest warriors. Many more lay bleeding and dying and the path back to uMgungundlovu was soon littered by the bodies of the wounded who could not complete the journey home.

Not one voortrekker was killed.

The direction of the Zulu attack at Blood river. (Robin Binckes)

From that day on no Zulu would drink the waters of the Ncomo river that was renamed Blood river, the battle known today as the battle of Blood river. The 16th of December came to be celebrated as a religous holiday by the Boers, to be known as the Day of the Vow, subsequently being changed to the Day of the Covenant, and known informally as Dingane's Day. Today in South Africa it is now the Day of Peace and Reconciliation. Regardless of the name, the 16th of December will always be remembered by the Afrikaners as the day that God protected the Boers from the enemy and they made Him a promise ... to honour the day as the Sabbath for ever.

14. THE END GAME

As the remnants of the Isihlangu Mnyama and Isihlangu Mhlopo limped back to uMgungundlovu a Boer commando under the command of Veld Kommandant Landman was in pursuit, shooting down the wounded and the stragglers. Occasionally some Zulu stragglers would put up a fight but resistance was futile until finally, as darkness descended, Landman and his commando returned to the laager at Blood river.

Umhlele realized that there was a strong likelihood of a Boer attack on the Zulu capital and sent out scouts to spy on their movements. The voortrekkers, who were indeed marching on uMgungundlovu, however identified and captured the scouts, executing them before they could warn Dingane of the commandos' approach.

On 20 December 1838 the Zulu at uMgungundlovu heard a shot. A small patrol of voortrekkers under Jacobus Uys, sent out by Pretorius to scout out the approach, had given their position away when Uys had foolishly fired a shot at a crow circling above. The sound of the shot alerted the entire Zulu army but, unwilling to engage in battle, Dingane ordered the burning of uMgungundlovu and the abandonment of the capital. Soon smoke filled the sky as the royal kraal was reduced to a pile of ash. Dingane fled.

A few days later when the voortrekkers were picking their way through the desolation looking for loot, they came across the bones of Piet Retief and his men on kwaMatiwane and discovered the agreement signed by Dingane in Retief's satchel that still hung from his rotting corpse. Not all the Zulu had fled and most were either captured or shot by the Boers. One of those captured—by design, to be sure—on Christmas Day was a Zulu *induna*, Bongoza, who after being interrogated by Pretorius, admitted that a number of Zulu were hiding in the valley of the White Umfolozi river, together with stolen Boer cattle not far from the voortrekker camp. Scanning the distance with a telescope, Pretorius was able to identify some 2,000 head of cattle in the valley far below.

On 27 December he ordered Kommandant Landman to take 300 voortrekkers and fifty 'friendly' Zulu to recover the cattle. Guided by Bongoza, the voortrekkers made their way down into the valley and as they looked down on the cattle, were astonished to see that the cattle appeared to be grouped by colour: the black oxen stood together

Today the founder of the Zulu nation lies buried beneath Couper street in the town of Stanger.

as did the white and red oxen. Suddenly an *impi* of 200 Zulu warriors appeared on the opposite side of the valley.

"That is all that is left of the Zulu army," Bongoza reassured Landman.

A shout was then heard: *"Izi pagati; izi pagati!"*—"They are inside; they are inside!"—and at that signal the 2,000 'cattle' stood up on their hind legs: the Zulus had been hiding under their shields and from above, as planned by Bongoza, they looked like cattle. Bongoza, realizing that the game was up, kicked his heels into the

A Zulu woman photographed on the road between Greytown and Dundee in the early 20th century. (Collectie Tropenmuseum)

side of his horse and with hands still bound galloped into the ranks of the approaching *impi* to make good his escape much to the chagrin of the furious Boers. For ten hours the voortrekkers fought the 2,000 warriors. Despite the Zulus losing almost half their number, the Boers sustained comparatively heavy losses: more than thirty friendly Zulu and seven Boers killed, as well as a significant number of wounded.

*

A few months later, Dingane's half-brother Mphande, 'the simple one', who had never liked Dingane, added to Dingane's woes by crossing over with 17,000 to 20,000 followers to seek protection from the voortrekkers, requesting to be allowed to settle between the Umvoti and Umhlali rivers. This was agreed to and the Boers swore in Mphande as the reigning prince of the emigrant Zulus with plans to install him as king of the Zulu once Dingane had been removed.

The great general Tambuza who had led the Isihlangu Mnyama at the battle of Blood river was taken prisoner and executed after visiting Pretorius bearing a message from Dingane. To his lasting shame, Pretorius was guilty of killing an emissary on a diplomatic mission.

On 30 January 1840, Mphande's warriors joined the Boers in a final battle against Dingane. Mphande's principal lieutenant, Nongalaza, was to defeat Dingane's army under the command of the loyal and brave Umhlele who had led the Isihlangu Mhlope at Blood river. After the battle, Dingane repaid Umhlele by personally strangling him with ox *riempie* (a leather strip) for the defeat by Nongalaza. Dingane then fled, seeking protection from the Swazis who in short order stabbed him to death.

So ended the bloodiest era in southern African history. It would be another forty years before Zulu might was to again manifest itself, this time against the imperial power of Britain, at a place called Isandhlwana.

NOTES

Introduction
1. Dan Wylie, *Myth of Iron*, pp. 68, 69.
2. Elizabeth A. Eldredge, *Kingdoms and Chiefdoms of Southeastern Africa: Oral Traditions and History, 1400–1830*, p. 154.

1. The Arrival of the Settlers
1. Author interview Chief Daniel Julius, 28 December 2017.
2. A. T. Bryant, *Olden Times in Zululand and Natal*, p. 82.
3. Ibid, p. 13.
4. Wylie, p. 25.
5. Ibid, p. 80.
6. Bird, p. 36
7. Bryant, p. 36.
8. Glen Lyndon Dodds, *The Zulus and Matabele: Warrior Nations*, p. 10.
9. Ibid, p. 11.

2. Shaka: The Quest for Power
1. *The Diary of Henry Francis Fynn*, p. 13.
2. John Laband, *Rope of Sand*, p. 17
3. Wylie, p. 157.
4. J. B. Peires, *The House of Phalo*, p. 88.
5. Fynn diary, p. 20.
6. Ibid. Page 22.
7. Bryant, p. 137.
8. Donald R. Morris, *The Washing of the Spears*, p. 54.
9. Ibid. Page 57
10. Eldredge, p. 200.
11. Rope of Sand. Page 19.
12. Eldredge, p. 204.
13. Bird, p. 65.

3. Matiwane's Path of Terror
1. Bryant, p. 140
2. Ibid, pp. 140, 141.
3. Ibid, pp. 142, 143.
4. Laband, p. 19
5. Ibid, p. 22.
6. Eldredge, p. 208.
7. Ian J. Knight, *Warrior Chiefs of Southern Africa*, p. 24, quote from Mangati kaGodide.
8. Ibid, p. 24, quote from Baleni kaSilwana.
9. Bryant, p. 206.
10. Wylie, p. 168

11. Laband, p. 24.
12. Knight, p. 25.
13. Laband, p. 30
14. Dodds, p. 25.

4. The British Arrive

1. Bird, p. 74.
2. Fynn diary, p. 88.
3. Knight, p. 34.
4. Fynn diary, p. 126.

5. Mzilikazi: The Bloodiest of All

1. Eldredge, p. 213.
2. Bryant, p. 608.
3. Fynn diary, pp. 134-136.
4. Peires, p. 87.
5. Morris, pp. 101, 102
6. Bryant, pp. 627-629.
7. Ibid, pp. 615-620, 656, 657

6. Dingane: Who Rules by Fear

1. Ibid, pp. 662-664.
2. Ibid, p. 668.
3. Fynn diary, pp. 156-160.
4. Bryant, p. 669.
5. Ibid, p. 671.
6. Ibid, pp. 144, 145.
7. Ibid, p. 428.

7. Mzilikazi's Rivers of Blood

1. *'Mlimo: The Rise and Fall of the Matabele*, Mziki (A.A. Campbell), pp. 51-53.
2. Bryant, pp. 424, 425
3. www.sahistory.org.za/people/king-mzilikazi
4. Ibid.
5. Dodds, p. 160.
6. www.sahistory.org.za/people/king-mzilikazi

8. Enter the Boers

1. Robin Binckes, *The Great Trek (Uncut)*, pp. 60-80.
2. Ibid, p. 202.

9. The Great Trek Begins

1. Ibid, pp. 247-253.

10. Defeat of the Matabele

1. Mziki (A.A. Campbell), p. 61.
2. Ibid, p. 61.
3. Ibid, p. 58.

4. Dodds, p. 168.
5. Ibid, p. 167.
6. Ibid, p. 169.
7. Ibid, p. 171.
8. Ibid, p. 172.

11. Intrusion onto the Land of the Zulu

1. Dr Ndlovu thesis 'Dingane'.

12. Weenen and Italeni

1. Binckes, pp. 342–344.

13. Blood River

1. Ibid, p. 366.

A fine portrayal of a Boer wagon outspanned. (Charles Davidson Bell)

BIBLIOGRAPHY

Archives Year Book for South African History Vol II, 1949

Becker, Peter, *Hill Of Destiny*, Longmans, 1965

_____, *Rule of Fear*, Longmans, London, 1964

Binckes, Robin, Great Trek (Uncut), 30° South Publishers, Durban, 2013

Bird, John, *Annals of Natal* Vol I, P. Davis & Sons, Pietermaritzburg

Boeseken, A.J., *Slaves and Free Blacks at the Cape, 1658–1700*, Tafelberg, Cape Town, 1977

Bryant, A. T., *History of the Zulu*, C. Struik, Cape Town, 1965

_____, *Olden Times in Zululand and Natal*, Longmans, Green & Co., London, 1929

Cape Archives, GR 1/9, letter from inhabitants of Zuurveld, 11 August 1788

Cory, George, *Owen's Diary*

_____, *Rise of South Africa* Vols l–V, Longmans, 1919

d'Assonville, V. E., *Blood River*, Marnix, 2000

Davenport, Rodney & Saunders, Christopher, *South Africa: A Modern History*, Palgrave Macmillan, 2000

De Jongh, P. S., *Sarel Cilliers*, Perskor, 1987

De Kock, Victor, *Those in Bondage*, George Allen & Unwin Ltd., London, 1950

The Diary of Erasmus Smit, C. Struik, Cape Town, 1972

Dodds, Glen Lyndon, *The Zulus and Matabele: Warrior Nations*, Arms & Armour Press, London, 1998

Dracopoli, J. L., *Sir Andries Stockenström*, A. A. Balkema, Cape Town, 1969

Eldredge, Elizabeth A., *Kingdoms and Chiefdoms of Southeastern Africa: Oral Traditions and History, 1400–1830*, University of Rochester Press, Rochester, 2015

Elphick, Richard & Gilomee, Herman, *The Shaping of South Africa*, Maskew Miller Longman, 1990

Elphick, Richard, *Kraal and Castle: Khoikhoi and the Founding of White South Africa*, Yale University Press, New Haven & London, 1977

Five Lectures, Delivered to the Natal Society at Pietermaritzburg by the Hon. Henry Cloete L.L.D., Recorder of the District

Franken, J. L. M., *Piet Retief: Sy Lewe in die Kolonie*, 1949

Gardiner, Allen Francis, *Narrative of a Journey to the Zoolu Country: In South Africa*, Struik, Cape Town, 1966

Genealogical Instituut van Zuid Afrika, Dutch Reformed Church Records

Gerdener, G.B.A., *Sarel Cilliers: Die Held van Vegkop*, J.L. van Schaik, Pretoria, 1925

_____, *Sarel Cilliers: Die Vader van Dingaansdag*. J.L. van Schaik, Pretoria, 1925.

Giliomee, Hermann & Mbenga, Bernard, *New History of South Africa*, Tafelberg, Cape Town, 2007

Gledhill, Eily & Jack, *In the Steps of Piet Retief*, Human & Rousseau, Cape Town, 1980

Heese, H. F., *Groep Sonder Grense, C-Reeks*, Navorsingpublikasies, 1984

Hockley, Harold Edward, *Story of the 1820 Settlers*, Juta, Cape Town, 1957

Holden, William Clifford, 'The Past and Future of the Kaffir Races', *Africana Collectanea* Vol III, C. Struik, Cape Town, 1963

Holden, William Clifford, *History of the Colony of Natal*, A. Heylin, London, 1855

Human Sciences Research Council. *Dictionary of South African* Biography, Vols I–V *Illustrated History of South Africa*: *The Real Story*, Reader's Digest, Cape Town, 1988

Internet reference: Marco Ramerini, 'The Dutch in South Africa, 1652–1795'

Internet site: www.tutufoundation.uk

Knight, Ian, *The Anatomy of the Zulu Army: From Shaka to Cetshwayo, 1818–1879*, Greenhill Books, London, 2006

_____, *The Sun Turned Black*, 2nd ed., William Waterman, South Africa, 1995

_____, *Warrior Chiefs of Southern Africa*, Firebird Books, New York City, 1994

Kotze, D. J., *Letters of the American Missionaries, 1835–1838*, Van Riebeeck Society, Cape Town, 1950

Laband, John, *Rope of Sand*, Jonathan Ball Publishers, Johannesburg, 1995

Le Roux, T. H., *Die Dagboek van Louis Trigardt*, J. L. van Schaik, Pretoria, 1966

Legassick, Martin, *The Struggle for the Eastern Cape, 1800–1854: Subjugation and the Roots of South African Democracy*, KMW Review Publishing Co., 2011

Lenta, Margaret & Le Cordeur, Basil, *The Cape Diaries of Lady Anne Barnard, 1799–1800* Vol I, Van Riebeeck Society, Cape Town, 1999

Liebenberg, B. J., *Andries Pretorius in Natal*, Academica, Pretoria, 1977

Mackeurten, Graham, *Cradle Days of Natal*, Shuter & Shooter, Pietermaritzburg, 1931

Macmillan, W. M., *Bantu, Boer and Briton*: *The Making of the South African Native Problem*, Faber & Gwyer, London

Meintjies, Johannes, *The voortrekkers*, Cassel, London, 1973

Mentzel, O. F., *Life at the Cape in the Mid-Eighteenth Century: The Biography of Rudolph Siegfried Alleman*, Van Riebeeck Society, Cape Town, 1919

Milton, John, *Edges of War: A History of Frontier Wars (1702–1878)*, Juta & Co., Ltd, Cape Town, 1983

Mitford-Barberton, Ivan, *Commandant Holden Bowker*, Human & Rosseau, Cape Town, 1970

Morris, Donald R., *Washing of the Spears*, Pimlico ed., London, 1965 & 1994

Mostert, Noël, *Frontiers*, Jonathan Cape, Pimlico ed., London, 1993

Muller, C. F. J., *Die Britse Owerheid en die Groot Trek*, Academika, 1948

_____, *Die Oorsprong van die Groot Trek*, Unisa Press, 1988

Mziki (Campbell, A. A.), *'Mlimo: The Rise and Fall of the Matabele*, Books of Rhodesia, Bulawayo, 1972

Nathan, Manfred, *The voortrekkers of South Africa*, Central News Agency Ltd. & Gordon & Gotch, Johannesburg,1937

Ndlovu, Sifiso Mxolisi, 'The Changing African Perceptions of King Dingane in Historical Literature', unpublished thesis, University of the Witwatersrand

Norval, E. J. G., *Bloed Sweet En Trane*, Bienedell Uitgewers, Pretoria, 2002

Peires, J. B., *The House of Phalo*, University of California Press, Los Angeles, 1982

Penn, Nigel, *The Forgotten Frontier*, Double Storey Books, Cape Town, 2005

Preller, Gustav, *Die Dagboek van Louis Trichardt*, 1918

_____, *voortrekkermense* Parts I & IV, Nasionale Pers, Cape Town, 1920 & 1938

_____, *Piet Retief*, Nasionale Pers, Cape Town, 1920

Pretorius, C. Celestine, *Op Trek*, Protea Boekhuis, Pretoria, 2008

Pringle, Thomas, *Narrative of a Residence in South Africa*, Edward Moxon, London, 1834 & Struik, Cape Town, 1966

Ransford, Oliver, *The Great Trek*, John Murray, London, 1972 & Cardinal Books, London (Birr), 1974

Raper, Peter E., & Boucher, Maurice, *Robert Jacob Gordon: Cape Travels, 1777–1786*, Brenthurst Press, Johannesburg, 1988

Raven-Hart, R., *Cape Good Hope*, A.A. Balkema, Cape Town, 1971

_____, *The Diary of Johann Jakob Merklein, 1653*, A.A. Balkema, Cape Town, 1971

_____, *Before Van Riebeeck: Callers at South Africa from 1488 to 1652*, C. Struik, Cape Town, 1967

Rivett-Carnac, D.E., *Hawk's Eye*, Howard Timmins, Cape Town, 1966

Sheffield. T., *The Story of the Settlement*, T.G. Sheffield, Grahamstown, 1882

Skotness, Pippa, *Claim to the Country: The Archive of Wilhelm Bleek and Lucy Lloyd*, Ohio University Press, Athens OH, 2007

Soga, John Henderson, *The Ama-Xosa: Life and Customs*, Lovedale Press, Alice

South African History On Line

Stuart, James & Malcolm, Daniel McK., *The Diary of Henry Francis Fynn*, Shuter & Shooter, Pietermaritzburg, 1969

Taylor, Stephen, *Shaka's Children*, Harper Collins, London 1994

Theal, George McCall, *Ethnography and Condition of South Africa before A.D. 1505*, G. Allen & Unwin Ltd., London, 1919

_____, *History and Ethnography of South Africa before 1795* Vols I–III, Swan Sonnenschein & Co., Bloomsbury, 1907

_____, *History of South Africa since 1795* Vols I–V, Swan Sonnenschein & Co., Lim, Bloomsbury, 1907

_____, *History of South Africa since 1795*, Vol II, Cambridge University Press, 2010

_____, *History of the Boers in South Africa*, Swan Sonnenschein & Co., London, 1888

Turner, Malcolm, *Shipwrecks and Salvage in South Africa, 1505 to the Present*, C. Struik, Cape Town, 1988

Van Warmelo, N. J., *History of Matiwane and the Amangwane Tribe*, Union of South Africa. Department of Native Affairs Blue Book, 1930

voortrekker Monument *Reeks* 1

Walker, Eric, *The Great Trek*, A.& C. Black Ltd., 1934

Welch, Sidney R., *South Africa under John III, 1521–1557*, Juta, Cape Town, 1948

Worden, Nigel; van Heyningen, Elizabeth & Bickford-Smith, Vivian, *The Making of a City*, David Philip, Cape Town, 1998

Wright, John Kirtland., *The Geographical Lore of the Time of the Crusades: A Study in the History of Medieval Science and Tradition in Western Europe*, American Geographical Society, Research Series No. 15, Literary Licensing, LLC, 2011

A Xhosa girl, Eastern Cape. (South African Tourism)

Index

A voortrekker dwelling. (British Library HMNTS 010093.i.20)

Robin Binckes was born in 1941 in the Eastern Cape, South Africa. Educated at Umtata in the Transkei, he enjoyed a business career that spanned Public Relations, sports promotion, travel and tourism and food retailing. He has written several historical books on South Africa, including the bestselling *The Great Trek—Escape from British Rule: The Boer Exodus from the Cape Colony, 1836*. He has recently started writing for several Pen & Sword military history series including 'History of Terror'. Inspired by the late David Rattray, he currently works in Johannesburg as a tour guide with his own company, Spear of the Nation, specializing in oratory story-telling.

Also by Robin Binckes

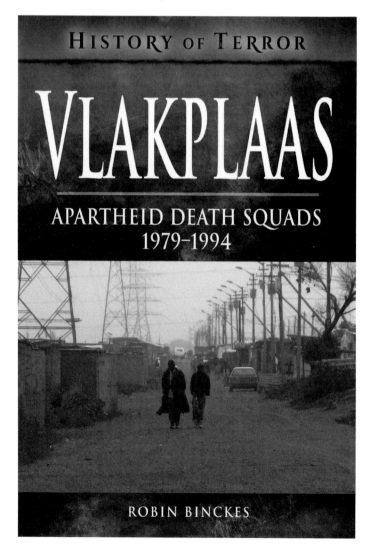